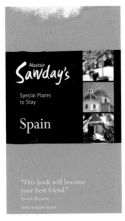

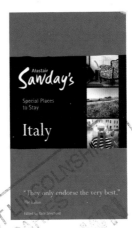

Alastair Sawday's

Special Places to Stay

First edition
Copyright © 2009 Alastair Sawday
Publishing Co. Ltd
Published in 2009
ISBN-13: 978-1-906136-15-4

Alastair Sawday Publishing Co. Ltd,
The Old Farmyard, Yanley Lane,
Long Ashton, Bristol BS41 9LR, UK
Tel: +44 (0)1275 395430
Email: info@sawdays.co.uk
Web: www.sawdays.co.uk

The Globe Pequot Press,
P. O. Box 480, Guilford,
Connecticut 06437, USA
Tel: +1 203 458 4500
Email: info@globepequot.com
Web: www.globepequot.com

Series Editor Alastair Sawday
Editor Kate Shepherd
Editorial Director Annie Shillito
Writing Jo Boissevain, Matthew Hilton-
Dennis, Honor Peters, Polly Procter,
Kate Shepherd
Inspections Georgina Gabriel, Marianne
Hablützel, Matthew Hilton-Dennis,
Katrin Hochberg, Ben Paine,
Fiona Schaller, Kate Shepherd
*Thanks also to those who did a few
inspections or a write-up or two.*
Accounts Bridget Bishop,
Amy Lancastle
Editorial Sue Bourner,
Jo Boissevain, Julie Monin, Polly Procter,
Cristina Sanchez Gonzalez, Lianka Varga
Production Jules Richardson,
Rachel Coe, Tom Germain
Sales & Marketing & PR
Rob Richardson,
Sarah Bolton, Bethan Riach, Lisa Walklin
Web & IT Joe Green,
Chris Banks, Phil Clarke, Mike Peake,
Russell Wilkinson

Maps: Maidenhead Cartographic Services
Printing: Butler Tanner & Dennis, Frome
UK distribution: Penguin UK, London

Alastair Sawday's

Special Places to Stay

Green Europe

4   Contents

The buildings

Beautiful as they were, our old offices leaked heat, used electricity to heat water and rooms, flooded spaces with light to illuminate one person, and were not ours to alter.

So in 2005 we created our own eco-offices by converting some old barns to create a low-emissions building. Heating and lighting the building, which houses over 30 employees, now produces only 0.28 tonnes of carbon dioxide per year. Not bad when you compare this with the 6 tonnes emitted by the average UK household. We achieved this through a variety of innovative and energy-saving building techniques, described below.

Insulation   We went to great lengths to ensure that very little heat will escape, by:
- laying insulating board 90mm thick immediately under the roof tiles and on the floor
- lining the whole of the inside of the building with plastic sheeting to ensure air-tightness
- fixing further insulation underneath the roof and between the rafters
- fixing insulated plaster-board to add another layer of insulation.

All this means we are insulated for the Arctic, and almost totally air-tight.

Heating   We installed a wood-pellet boiler from Austria, in order to be largely fossil-fuel free. The pellets are made from compressed sawdust, a waste product from timber mills that work only with sustainably managed forests. The heat is conveyed by water to all corners of the building via an under-floor system.

Water   We installed a 6000-litre tank to collect rainwater from the roofs. This is pumped back, via an ultra-violet filter, to the lavatories, showers and basins. There are two solar thermal panels on the roof providing heat to the one (massively insulated) hot-water cylinder.

Lighting   We have a carefully planned mix of low-energy lighting: task lighting and up-lighting. We also installed three sun-pipes — polished aluminium tubes that reflect the outside light down to chosen areas of the building.

Electricity   All our electricity has long come from the Good Energy Company and is 100% renewable.

Materials   Virtually all materials are non-toxic or natural. Our carpets, for example, are made from (80%) Herdwick sheep-wool from National Trust farms in the Lake District.

Doors and windows   Outside doors and new windows are wooden, double-glazed, beautifully constructed in Norway. Old windows have been double-glazed.

We have a building we are proud of, and architects and designers are fascinated by. But best of all, we are now in a better position to encourage our owners and readers to take sustainability more seriously.

Photo: Tom Germain

What we do

Besides moving the business to a low-carbon building, the company works in a number of ways to reduce its overall environmental footprint:

- all office travel is logged as part of a carbon sequestration programme, and money for compensatory tree-planting is dispatched to SCAD in India for a tree-planting and development project
- we avoid flying and take the train for business trips wherever possible; when we have to fly, we 'double offset'
- car-sharing and the use of a company pool car are part of company policy; recycled cooking oil is used in one car and LPG in the other
- organic and fairtrade basic provisions are used in the staff kitchen and organic food is provided by the company at all in-house events
- green cleaning products are used throughout the office
- all kitchen waste is composted and used on the office organic allotment.

Our total 'operational' carbon footprint (including travel to and from work, plus all our trips to visit our Special Places to Stay) is just over 17 tonnes per year. We have come a long way, but we would like to get this figure as close to zero as possible.

For many years Alastair Sawday Publishing has been 'greening' the business in different ways. Our aim is to reduce our environmental footprint as far as possible – with almost everything we do we have the environmental implications in mind. (We once claimed to be the world's first carbon-neutral publishing company, but are now wary of such claims.) In recognition of our efforts we won a Business Commitment to the Environment Award in 2005, and in 2006 a Queen's Award for Enterprise in the Sustainable Development category. In that year Alastair was voted ITN's 'Eco Hero'.

We have created our own eco-offices by converting former barns to create a low-emissions building. Through a variety of innovative and energy-saving techniques this has reduced our carbon emissions by 35%.

Photo: Tom Germain

But becoming 'green' is a journey and, although we began long before most companies, we still have a long way to go.

In 2008 and again in 2009 we won the Independent Publishers Guild Environmental Award. The judging panel were effusive in their praise, stating: "With green issues currently at the forefront of publishers' minds, Alastair Sawday Publishing was singled out in this category as a model for all independents to follow. Its efforts to reduce waste in its office and supply chain have reduced the company's environmental impact, and it works closely with staff to identify more areas of improvement. Here is a publisher who lives and breathes green. Alastair Sawday has all the right principles and is clearly committed to improving its practice further."

Our Fragile Earth series is a growing collection of campaigning books about the environment. Highlighting the perilous state of the world yet offering imaginative and radical solutions and some intriguing facts, these books will make you weep and smile. They will keep you up to date and well armed for the battle with apathy.

THE QUEEN'S AWARDS
FOR ENTERPRISE:
SUSTAINABLE DEVELOPMENT
2006

ipa⁰⁹

"Large scale monocultures have left us with 75 per cent of the world's food being grown from only 12 plant types and five animal species."

Andrew Simms, *Nine Meals from Anarchy*, New Economics Foundation

If you have travelled through the great grain-producing swathes of Northern France, you will understand the above – another grim warning about the many threats to our survival. Europe, rich and dynamic as it is, is no safer than anywhere else, though perhaps the worst will come to us later than to most.

Europe has been the main focus for our publishing. We kicked off the series with *French Bed & Breakfast*, then came *Britain*, followed by books on Spain, Ireland, Portugal, Italy, Turkey, Greece – and finally Croatia. It has been frustrating not to reach the many other countries of Europe, but this extraordinary book is the answer. We chose only to include the places that are impressive for their commitment to making the world a greener, and better, place. That sets the book apart from others right away, apart from our own world-wide *Green Places to Stay*.

Recent surveys on attitudes to travel show a remarkable turnaround – over 70% of us now agree, for example, that airlines should pay the environmental costs of flying. The surge in interest in all things green is palpable, undeniable, uplifting. Green tourism awards are

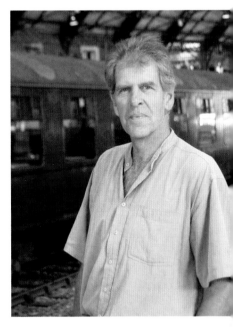

being designed and launched by tourism authorities all over Europe, some superb and others, admittedly, little more than 'greenwash'. It is hard for conscientious travellers to know how to make meaningful choices. I believe that *Green Europe* is one answer.

Almost anyone asked to choose between a beautiful green hotel and an equally beautiful non-green one would choose the former. Choose these places, and make a real, albeit tiny, contribution to the health of our planet. Most of the people in this book are fascinating, so the chances are that you will be getting far more out of them than just a comfortable night.

Alastair Sawday

The adoption of 'green' by eco-centric political parties and activist groups in the 1970s marked the beginning of a universal new meaning. 'Green' aptly responded to a growing distaste for the 'greyness' of industrialisation and lifeless concrete monotonously consuming fields and wildlife habitats, and its message could be carried without further comment; associated with grass, leaves, plants, trees it is a representative of Nature, and flying her flag raised the awareness of biospheric health around the globe.

But what does it mean to 'go green', apart from acknowledging the fragility of Nature and a responsibility to protect it? Compiling this guide has put me in touch with aspiring greenies throughout Europe and their answers to this question have been as varied as the countries of Europe themselves. The organic farmers and conservationists are green thanks to their protection of biodiversity; the vegetarians because their meat-free living decreases cow-produced methane and deforestation for animal feed. Investors in renewable energy are green saviours for diminishing dependency on fossil fuels and there are those who are green just for swapping their lightbulbs, recycling their newspaper; or simply because they say so (one person even claimed to be green for living in the countryside).

This book includes those on the zenith of the Continent, Arctic dwellers living under the mystique of the Northern Lights; the Atlantic representatives, in an epic range from Iceland to Portugal; the land-locked Germanic descendents; and, from Spain to Greece, the hot-blooded Mediterraneans. Listening attentively to the meaning of green to people living in such a cross section of places I have been intensely aware of the evolution of the green movement and the uncertain attempts of so many to understand the most appropriate (and realistic) way to follow it.

The truth is, there are very few people in Europe who are able to lead, or know how to lead, a 100% Nature-friendly lifestyle. You may have converted to organic food but solar panels are forbidden on your listed building; you're running entirely off-grid but you haven't the time for biodynamic farming; you have pioneered a conservation project but your kitchen has an oil-fuelled Aga. In this guide, one of the

Photo left: The Peren, entry 21
Photo right: Perché dans le Perche, entry 62

first of its kind, all these owners have been included alongside those who are more ardently green. Nobody has been included who doesn't continuously seek improvements in what they do. The places in this guide have another crucial element in common: all allow visitors to leave feeling stimulated, motivated, encouraged, moved, even inspired, by an ecological way of life, whether it be after a stay in an environmentally sustainable hut in Wales, a conservation project in Greece, an organic hotel in Denmark or a biodynamic farm in Italy.

If your expectation of a green place to stay is a primitive cabin in the forest, a tree house or a super-modern eco-chic home – those I call the über-green places – you won't be disappointed for there are plenty here. But this is Europe so it would be unnatural if it lacked historic castles, villas and traditional family homes. From the simple to the most elegant, all those included fulfil our criteria for what is special and all deserve recognition for their green efforts.

While most Sawday owners are acutely aware of avoiding eco preach over breakfast, with their stories of finding the best insulation or campaigning for local solar they could be a fantastic resource for being greener at home: it's worth picking your hosts' brains if you can. Most owners can also advise on arrival by public transport. (Although I recommend Time Out's *Flight-Free Europe* and the excellent www.greentraveller.co.uk; the latter provides a forum where no green travel question goes unanswered.) Remember that the green experience also depends upon your own personal green input… forewarning friends in your self-catering party that it's a green holiday (following everyone around checking they are recycling is no-one's idea of fun) and avoiding using standard shampoos (most places will reuse your water to feed the garden and encourage wildlife) are all too easy to forget about. Try to keep in mind that you may be part of an exciting 'ecosystem', a cycle that depends upon entirely natural processes. It's worth reminding yourself of a few simple green guidelines, and, if you're unsure, ask your host – they should provide you with all the information you need and even divulge a hidden wildlife habitat encouraged partly because of your stay.

Finally, if you are wondering what on earth a ground-source heat pump or a reed bed sewage system is, or if you come across any other unfamiliar eco speak in the descriptions, I've provided a short glossary of terms at the back of the guide.

Green Europe is the responsibility of us all – inhabitants and visitors alike. Using this book brings you one step closer to taking that responsibility: one small step for green, a giant leap for Nature.

Kate Shepherd

It's simple. There are no rules, no clipboards. We choose places that we like and are fiercely subjective in our choices. We also recognise that one person's idea of special is not necessarily someone else's so there is a huge variety of places, and prices, in the book. Those who are familiar with our Special Places series know that we look for comfort, originality, authenticity, and reject the insincere, the anonymous and the banal. The way guests are treated comes as high on our list as the setting, the architecture, the atmosphere and the food.

Every place in this book is also part of our series-wide "Ethical Collection"; the owners have all completed a detailed questionnaire to explain how they are working to reduce their environmental footprint, make significant contributions to their local community, or source local or organic food – for more information see page 211. Do ask owners about their 'green efforts' – often the work is entirely behind the scenes, and they can explain how the business is converted into a training centre for youths during winter months, give you a tour of the organic vegetable garden supplying the hotel restaurant, or show you the extent of the solar panels on the roof.

Inspections

We visit every place in the guide to get a feel for how both house and owner tick. Our inspections are informal – we chat for an hour or so with the owner and look round, giving us an excellent idea of

who would enjoy staying there. Green inspections often involve a fascinating tour, perhaps of recycling stations, organic gardens, biomass boilers, conservation sites – even the odd loft or two to check out natural insulation. If the visit happens to be the last of the day, we sometimes stay the night. Once in the book, properties are re-inspected every three to four years so that we can keep things fresh and accurate.

Feedback

In between inspections we rely on feedback from our army of readers, as well as from staff members who are encouraged to visit properties across the series. This feedback is invaluable to us and we always follow up on comments.

Photo: Hotel Balance, entry 95

So do tell us whether your stay has been a joy or not, if the atmosphere was great or stuffy, the owners cheery or bored. The accuracy of the book depends on what you, and our inspectors, tell us. A lot of the new entries in each edition are recommended by our readers, so keep telling us about new places you've discovered too. Please use the forms on our website at www.sawdays.co.uk, or write to us.

However, please do not tell us if the bedside light was broken, or the shower head was scummy. Tell the owner, immediately, and get them to do something about it. Most owners are more than happy to correct problems and will bend over backwards to help. Far better than bottling it up and then writing to us a week later!

Subscriptions

Owners pay to appear in this guide. Their fee goes towards the high costs of inspecting, of producing an all-colour book and of maintaining our website. We only include green places that we like and find special for one reason or another, so it is not possible for anyone to buy their way onto these pages. Nor is it possible for the owner to write their own description. We will say if the bedrooms are small, or if a main road is near. We do our best to avoid misleading people.

Disclaimer

We make no claims to pure objectivity in choosing these places. They are here simply because we like them. Our opinions and tastes are ours alone and this book is a statement of them; we hope you will share them. We have done our utmost to get our facts right but apologise unreservedly for any mistakes that may have crept in.

You should know that we don't check such things as fire regulations, swimming pool security or any other laws with which owners of properties receiving paying guests should comply. This is the responsibility of the owners.

Photo above: Kolarbyn Eco-Lodge, entry 121
Photo right: Oriel Gwyr, entry 37

you will be comfortable. If something is particularly important to you then check when you book: a simple question or two can avoid misunderstandings.

Maps

Each property is flagged with its entry number on the maps at the front. These maps are a great starting point for planning your trip, but please don't use them as anything other than a general guide – use a decent road map for real navigation. Most places will send you detailed instructions once you have booked your stay.

Finding the right place for you

All these places are green and special in one way or another. All have been visited and then written about honestly so that you can decide for yourselves which will suit you. Those of you who swear by Sawday's books trust our write-ups precisely because we don't have a blanket standard; we include places simply because we like them. But we all have different priorities, so do read the descriptions carefully and pick out the places where

Symbols

Below each entry you will see some symbols, which are explained at the very back of the book. They are based on the information given to us by the owners. However, things do change: bikes may be under repair or the owners have a new pet. Please use the symbols as a guide rather than an absolute statement of fact and double-check anything that is important to you – owners occasionally bend their own rules, so it's worth asking if you may take your child or dog even if they don't have the symbol.

Swimming pools – We're aware that swimming pools use large amounts of water, require huge amounts of energy to heat and are often chemically treated to ensure they meet health and safety requirements. We have tried to include only natural pools, like the one

Photo top: Hotel Kürschner, entry 98
Photo bottom: La Métairie, entry 60

at Hotel Balance in Switzerland (entry 95), or pools whose overflows feed the garden (Agriturismo La Faula in Italy, entry 156), but all-organic farms with "normal" pools have been included too.

Air-conditioning – Most of the places selected for this book recognize the amount of precious energy that air conditioning uses, but in some parts of Europe travellers rely more on air-conditioning so we have marked those places that provide it.

Children – The 🎈 symbol shows places which are happy to accept children of all ages. This does not mean that they will necessarily have cots, high chairs, etc. If an owner welcomes children but only those above a certain age, we have put these details at the end of their write-up. These houses do not have the child symbol, but even these folk may accept your younger child if you are the only guests. Many who say no to children do so not because they don't like them but because they may have a steep stair, an unfenced pond or they find balancing the needs of mixed age groups too challenging.

Pets – Our 🐕 symbol shows places which are happy to accept pets. It means they can sleep in the bedroom with you, but not on the bed. Be realistic about your pet – if it is nervous or excitable or doesn't like the company of other dogs, people, chickens, or children, then say so.

Owners' pets – The 🐈 symbol is given when the owners have their own pet on the premises. It may not be a cat! But it is there to warn you that you may be greeted by a dog, serenaded by a parrot, or indeed sat upon by a cat.

Quick reference indices

At the back of the book you'll find a number of quick-reference indices showing those places that offer a particular service, perhaps a room for under £70/€100 a night, or that are particularly good for vegetarians. They are worth flicking through if you are looking for something specific.

Photo: L'Aubier: Le Café-Hôtel, entry 97

Types of places

This book covers all types of places to stay, as long as they are special, and green. The type of place is indicated on each entry, and an outline of what we mean by each type is given below.

B&Bs – range from people's homes, where you can enjoy a glimpse of family life, through to guest houses with receptionists. And many B&Bs – in addition to the wonderful breakfasts – offer first-class food in the evenings. Some owners give you a front door key so you may come and go as you please; others like to have the house empty between, say, 10am and 4pm.

Hotels – come in all sorts too, from the country-house hotel with touches of luxury and lots of services, to the little modern place in town where the emphasis is on intimacy and hands-on attention. Food is nearly always a feature, often the best local/organic produce.

Self-catering – we use this to describe anywhere, from a cottage in Ireland to a hut in Sweden, where you can cook for yourself. Most self-catering places can be rented by the week, but an increasing number offer short breaks, or even overnight stays. Always check for additional costs such as linen at self-catering places.

Rooms

Bedrooms – We tell you if a room is a double, twin/double (ie with zip and link beds), suite (with a sitting area), family or single. Owners will usually be flexible if they can and juggle beds or bedrooms; talk to them about what you need before you book. It is rare to be given your own room key in a B&B. Where an entry reads '3 + 1' this means 3 B&B rooms plus 1 self-catering apartment/cottage.

Bathrooms – Most bedrooms in this book have an en suite bath or shower room; we only mention bathroom details when they do not. If these things are important to you, please check when booking.

Meals

Apart from at self-catering properties, a breakfast is included unless we say otherwise. Often you will feast on local sausage and bacon, eggs from resident hens, homemade breads and jams. Sometimes you may have organic yogurts and beautifully presented fruit compotes. Other places will give you a good continental breakfast instead. Some places are fairly unbending about breakfast times, others are happy to just wait until you want it, or even bring it to you in bed.

Photo: Le Camp, entry 86

Apart from breakfast, no meals should be expected unless you have arranged them in advance. Meal prices are quoted per person, and at B&Bs dinner is often a social occasion shared with your hosts and other guests.

Do eat in if you can – this book is teeming with good cooks. And how much more relaxing after a day out to have to move no further than the dining room for an excellent dinner, and to eat and drink knowing there's only a flight of stairs between you and your bed.

Prices and minimum stays

The prices we quote are per night per room unless otherwise stated, breakfast included. For self-catering we specify if the price is per week; for half-board it may be per person (p.p.). Meal prices are always given per person.

Price ranges cover seasonal differences and different types of rooms. Some owners charge more at certain times (during festivals, for example) and some charge less for stays of more than one night. Some ask for a two-night minimum stay at weekends or in high season, and we mention this where possible. Prices quoted are those given to us for 2009–2011 but are not guaranteed, so do double-check when booking. Prices are given in local currencies, but we've given an approximate price band for comparison.

Booking and cancellation

Requests for deposits vary; some are non-refundable, and some owners may charge you for the whole of the booked stay in advance.

Some cancellation policies are more stringent than others. It is also worth noting that some owners will take this deposit directly from your credit/debit card without contacting you to discuss it. So ask them to explain their cancellation policy clearly before booking so you understand exactly where you stand; it may well avoid a nasty surprise.

Payment

The majority of places take credit or debit cards, but do check in advance that your particular card is acceptable. Those places that do not take cards are marked with a cash/cheque symbol.

Tipping

Owners do not expect tips. If you have been treated with extraordinary kindness, write to them, or leave a small gift. Please tell us, too – we love to hear, and we do note, all feedback.

Arrivals and departures

In hotels rooms are usually available by mid-afternoon; in B&Bs and self-catering places it may be a bit later, but do try and agree an arrival time with the owners in advance or you may find nobody there.

Closed

When given in months this means the whole of the month(s) stated. So, 'Closed: November–March' means closed from 1 November to 31 March.

With our existing especially green places and a handful of new recommendations from Sawday travellers in the back pocket, the hunt was on to find even more green places to stay. And in our enthusiasm for this exciting new guide, looking under the European Eco-label seemed a fine place to start. Set up by the European Commission as an independent arbiter of all things green in Europe, it has a growing list of places to stay that meet strict environmental criteria. The listings of the Green Key (*La Clef Verte*), too, brightened our day. Then there was Britain's Green Tourism Business Scheme, the Nordic Swan ecolabel, and the biodynamic Demeter Certification… Europe, happily, has a growing number of eco-friendly holidays to choose from.

But green labels have just one function: to help us make informed choices and spend our money in more environmentally friendly ways. Labels don't distinguish between kind and intelligent hosts and less welcoming greenies, or between organic meals cooked with love and care and those churned out for profit. The challenge for this book was not in finding green places to stay but in finding special places to stay that were also green.

'Green' and 'special' may sound vague, but the moment you experience somewhere that unites the two, you feel the pleasure. Take the solar-powered, zero-impact Chalet Châtelet in the French Alps, run by a delightful and cultured pair who also cook delicious organic food. Or Oriel Gwyr, a holiday home on a conservation stretch of the rugged Welsh coast, with an amazing turf roof and a chunky dining table made of reclaimed wood. Or L'Aubier: Le Café-Hôtel, in the centre of an old Swiss village, with bright inviting bedrooms upstairs and a bohemian café below, supplied by a neighbouring biodynamic farm.

Our idea of special is, necessarily, subjective (see page 13) and our green selections are subjective too (page 211). The result is a broad mix of sustainability, biodiversity, conservation and restoration each with a good dose of inspiration (and often unaccompanied by the green labels mentioned above). Monsieur and Madame Fussler's fortified bastide B&B in Provence is not a typical green place to stay but, for an ancient place where Templars once roamed, its ground-source heat pump and impressive water recycling system make it a fantastic and very special entry. Carrick's at Castle Farm, a B&B in Norfolk, caught our conservation eye for the part it's played in DEFRA's Higher Level Stewardship Scheme (as well as for providing binoculars in every bedroom for the birdlife), while the 600-year-old Pálacio Belmonte in Lisbon is included for the owner's campaign to change Portuguese conservation laws to continue with his impressive use of lime in restoration.

Our special organic and biodynamic farms have been selected not only for their promotion of biodiversity but because they are doing something different, or are working for the wider benefit of the community. Take Hof Klostersee in Germany, whose owners get a thumbs-up for having converted one of their barns into a home for the elderly; Château Haut Garrigue, a superb organic vineyard near Bergerac; or Jessenhofke in Belgium, where you can try the owner's own organic brews – and, if you time it right, be a brewer for a day.

And finally the über-greens, with their tiny impact on the environment and huge impact on the imagination; choose from a selection of absurdly special places such as tipis, treehouses, yurts and forest huts dotted lightly across Europe's richly varied soil.

If you're wondering why Eastern Europe or even some Western European countries have not been included, please don't assume it's because they aren't making steps in the green direction. Indeed, many Eastern European countries are inherently organic, having never succumbed to the use of chemicals on their farms, but for this first edition we had to draw a line after sixteen European countries to get the book to you at all. If you have any special green recommendations in the countries we have not included we'd love to hear from you – the more green places to stay there are in the public eye,

the better chance there is of others following suit.

By visiting the European countries included in the guide we have discovered a huge variety of green approaches, and if you stay in the places we recommend you'll get a fascinating insight into a range of contemporary green lifestyles. Find out, for example, how a hotel owner runs a large eco-friendly business in Britain while keeping things personal (Strattons); how an Italian farmer copes with labour-intensive organic farming (Giravento); how an eco-architect in France has created an inspirational living space (Earthship Perrine); or how a modest family in Austria leads a happily green life (Haus Troth).

Whatever your previous experience of green places to stay, in this guide green and special are united. We hope you enjoy the selection.

Photo: Ullershov Gård, entry 117

Catered properties
Self-catering properties
Mix of catered/self-catering

0   40   80 kilometres
0   30   60 miles

Map 2   25

© Maidenhead Cartographic 2009

© Maidenhead Cartographic 2009

Map 4   27

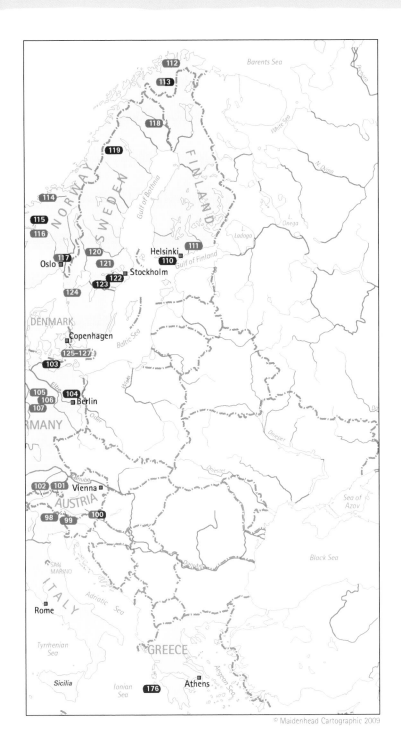

© Maidenhead Cartographic 2009

© Maidenhead Cartographic 2009

Map 6   29

There is something tantalising about the great train stations of Europe. As you enter the grand Stazione Centrale di Milano, with its neo-classical façade, it's hard not to be swept up by the history and the romance. The Italian Futurists were equally enamoured and used the station as their muse. For them, rail travel represented dynamism and progression, both of the individual and society; and the station signified a timeless realm where past and future met. Hopes and aspirations hung on the emotions of those who came and went, and there's no doubt you can sense that excitement still, in the grand old stations of Europe.

Part of Europe's charm lies in the diversity of its countries and their proximity to each other. There's no more liberating way to experience this than by train, and the excitement you feel as you pull into each station is enhanced by the anticipation that the next port of call might be Berlin, Lisbon, Paris or Rome.

When the London Eurostar terminal opened at St Pancras in 2007, the European media hailed a new Golden Age of rail and people were inspired by the opportunity to reach Europe in an eco-friendly way. But there's more to it than that. Such travel allows you to savour the experience of travel itself: the stations and the sensations, the landscapes and the people; cabins on sleeper trains, breakfast in the dining car, a good book or a game of chess as Europe flashes past the window; trains that board ferries on the Baltic sea, forcing you on to the top deck for biscuits and tea. The Futurists of the 1920s may have celebrated speed but today's trains are all about going slow.

If you are thinking of travelling to and around Europe by train we recommend an InterRail (or Eurail) pass. It will give you flexibility, so that, at no extra cost, you can travel to Austria and stop off in Belgium on the way. (We have marked with the symbol 🚂 all our places to stay that lie within ten miles of a station and where owners are happy to arrange pick up.) Roaming tickets will also encourage you to taste some of Europe's finest railway journeys: the Glacier Express in Switzerland, the Al Andalus Express in Andalucia, the Bergen Express in Norway. If you do happen to pull into Milan's Central Station on one of your travels, why not leave your bags in left-luggage and head off to the city's Civico Museo d'Arte Contemporanea – see for yourself if the Futurist paintings capture the excitement you felt on arrival at one of Europe's great stations.

- www.seat61.com offers fantastic advice on fares and bookings for European sea and land travel
- www.raileurope.co.uk is the place to book tickets

Britain & Ireland

Trelowarren

Cornwall without the crush. Deep in woodland, a mile from any road, 19 eco cottages sit in one of Europe's top five botanical sites in a mystical Celtic land of serene coves and sun-dappled creeks. The truly visionary Sir Ferrers is creating a natural paradise – one that not only his five young sons will be proud of but the wider community, too. His aim is self-sufficiency – in food and fuel – and he hopes to supply chef Greg Laskey with 70-80,000 tonnes of organic fruit and veg each year (reluctant self-caterers note: no need to cook *anything*!). Paints are organic and high-spec showers and baths are fed with reclaimed rainwater and heated by a woodchip burner using coppiced wood from the surrounding trees. But there is tangible comfort for the sybarite… Heals' tables, leather sofas, Conran crockery, ash floors, superb beds and cotton linen. There's even a pool. Children can explore a vaulted chamber or go with the gamekeeper on a dusk wildlife walk. You'll be hard-pushed to find a more alluring choice for gatherings of family or friends.

Price	From £450 per week for 4.
Rooms	19 cottages: 1 for 4, 4 for 3-4, 2 for 6, 11 for 6-8, 1 for 8-10.
Meals	Lunch from £6.95. Dinner, 3 courses, from £22.95. Wine from £15.50.
Closed	Never.
Directions	From Helston, A3083 towards Culdrose; pass Culdrose & left on B3293 for about 1.5 miles. At top of hill 3rd exit (not Mawgan village), pass Garras school then left, signed.

Ethical Collection: Environment.
See page 211.

Price band: C

Mrs Anne Coombes
Trelowarren,
Mawgan, Helston,
Cornwall TR12 6AF

Tel	+44 (0)1326 221224
Email	info@trelowarren.com
Web	www.trelowarren.com

The Hen House

Sandy and Gary, truly welcoming, are passionately committed to sustainability and love guiding you to the best places to eat, visit, cycle and walk – and there are OS maps on loan for hikers. Sandy teaches sustainable tourism to local businesses (they've reduced The Hen House emissions by 30% thanks to better light bulbs) and, with boundless positive energy, Gary is setting up a local farmers' market. Hand-harvested serpentine clads the new extensions, butts collect every drop of water for the garden. Enlightened souls will adore the spacious, colourful rooms, the bright fabrics, the wildflower meadow with inviting sunloungers, the pond, the tai chi, the fairy-lit courtyard at night, the scrumptious local food, the birdsong. There's even a sanctuary room for reiki and reflexology set deep into the earth. Recyling goes above and beyond: a yew tree destined for firewood is now a wardrobe; the garden path and dining room steps, a felled ash tree that had died. Sandy and Gary are spreading the green message throughout Cornwall – it's infectious.

Price	£70–£80. Singles £60. Barn £200–£450 per week.
Rooms	2 + 1: 2 doubles. Barn for 2.
Meals	Pub/restaurant 1 mile.
Closed	Rarely.
Directions	A3083 from Helston, then B3293 to St Keverne; left to Newtown-in-St Martin. After 2 miles, right at T-junc. Follow road for 2.3 miles then left fork. Round 7 bends then right at triangulation stone for Tregarne.

Sandy & Gary Pulfrey
The Hen House,
Tregarne, Manaccan, Helston,
Cornwall TR12 6EW

Tel	+44 (0)1326 280236
Email	henhouseuk@aol.com
Web	www.thehenhouse-cornwall.co.uk

Ethical Collection: Environment; Food.
See page 211.

Price band: C

Primrose Valley Hotel

Roll out of bed, drop down for breakfast, slip off to the beach, stroll into town. If you want St Ives bang on your doorstep, you'll be hard pressed to find a better hotel; the sands are a 30-second stroll. Half the rooms have views across the bay, two have balconies for lazy afternoons. Inside, open-plan interiors revel in an earthy contemporary chic, with leather sofas, varnished floors, fresh flowers and glossy magazines. Bedrooms tend not to be large but you can't fault the price or the style. There are Hypnos beds, bespoke furniture and all-natural soaps in super bathrooms; the suite, with its red leather sofa, hi-tech gadgetry and mind-blowing bathroom, is seriously fancy. Owners Andrew and Sue are proactively reducing the hotel's impact; recycling is de rigueur and green energy powers the lights. Their hugely popular breakfast is mostly sourced within the county, food provenance is listed on the menu and the 'visitor payback scheme' has raised thousands for the Marine Conservation Society. Indulge in the new wellness room with its fairtrade cotton towels and all-natural products. A treat. *Discount if you leave the car at home.*

Price	£105–£175. Suite £200–£235.
Rooms	9: 6 doubles, 2 twins, 1 suite.
Meals	Platters £8. Wine £12–£48. Restaurant 200m.
Closed	23-27 December; 3-29 January.
Directions	From A3074 Trelyon Avenue; before hospital sign slow down, indicate right & turn down Primrose Valley; under bridge, left, then back under bridge; signs for hotel parking.

Ethical Collection: Environment; Food. See page 211.

Price band: E

Andrew & Sue Biss
Primrose Valley Hotel,
Primrose Valley, Porthminster Beach,
St Ives, Cornwall TR26 2ED

Tel	+44 (0)1736 794939
Email	info@primroseonline.co.uk
Web	www.primroseonline.co.uk

Organic Panda B&B & Gallery

Organic by name, organic by nature. A five-minute walk from busy artistic St Ives, with a panoramic view of the bay, is a B&B in perfect harmony with this spot. Come for a bold scattering of modern art and beautiful furniture including a ten-seater rustic table made from reclaimed wood: perfect for convivial breakfasts. Spacious contemporary bedrooms swaddled in woollen insulation have a laid-back boutique style with their organic linen, bamboo towels, chunky beds, white walls and raw-silk cushions... ask for a sea view. Warm lighting is low-energy, electricity comes from green sources and the art is for sale. Shower rooms are small but perfectly formed, and smell sweetly of Faith in Nature or Avalon Organics treats. Andrea is an artist and theatre designer, Peter is a photographer, chef and Slow Food member – breakfasts are stunning and the menu suits all. Wake to the smell of fresh bread and organic regional produce meticulously sourced, then head for Porthminster Beach – or the glorious coastal road to St Just. Peter and Andrea's next venture is an organic deli – the first in St Ives.

Price	£75–£120.
Rooms	3: 2 doubles, 1 twin.
Meals	Packed lunch £10. Restaurants nearby.
Closed	Rarely.
Directions	A3074 to St Ives. Signs to leisure centre; house behind 3rd sign, on left-hand bend.

Peter Williams & Andrea Carr
Organic Panda B&B & Gallery,
1 Pednolver Terrace, St Ives,
Cornwall TR26 2EL

Tel   +44 (0)1736 793890
Email   info@organicpanda.co.uk
Web   www.organicpanda.co.uk

Ethical Collection: Environment; Food.
See page 211.

Price band: D

Rosehill Lodges

Modernity without mediocrity: these elegant lodges follow the path of the on-site stream down a valley that fans out into Porthtowan beach – one of the most sublime on the North Cornwall coast. Each lodge is topped with a mop of turf roof: on some, the grass hangs like a hippy hairdo. Within, the Cornish larch from which the lodges are built stands proud. Packed with mod cons (from granite breakfast bars to 'personal hot tub spas' on the decking), they are impeccably well turned out. As if this were not special enough, they are also built and maintained with sustainability at heart. The insulation is remarkable, the floors are bamboo, the lights low-energy, the water solar-warmed and you won't forget to recycle your rubbish: there are compartmentalised bins outside every front door. Owners and creators John and Pauline have been recycling since the days they had to pay to do it, such is their single-mindedness. Stroll from your lodge to the beach where you can even dine green: the Blue Bar has recently won its own Green Tourism award. Luxury goes green. *Minimum stay three nights.*

Price	£482-£1,580 for 4. £539-£1,878 for 6. Prices per week.
Rooms	10 lodges: 6 for 4, 4 for 6.
Meals	Restaurant within walking distance.
Closed	Never.
Directions	Leave A30 dir. Penzance at exit for St Agnes (B2377). Next r'bout 3rd exit (B3277), then left to Porthtowan. Straight over crossroads, then down hill, past beach turning; left into driveway 300 yds on.

Ethical Collection: Environment.
See page 211.

Price band: D

	Rebecca Vickerstaff
	Rosehill Lodges, Porthtowan, Cornwall TR4 8AR
Tel	+44 (0)1209 891920
Email	reception@rosehilllodges.com
Web	www.rosehilllodges.com

Coriander Cottages: Badger's Hollow

No shortage of natural entertainment here: a buzzard hovering overhead, a gaggle of waddling ducks, a night-time display by bats, a private terrace to ensure a ringside view. For a deep-country setting, this former cider barn, in the grounds of a converted water mill, is surprisingly lively. The Kings moved to the mill in search of peace and a greener way of life. Their former life as hoteliers shows: the barn combines its ultra-green credentials with luxury. Solar panels and geothermal heat ensure energy is renewable, rainwater is harvested and a flurry of organic materials keeps everything harmonious. An open-plan living space, sleek with limestone flooring, wooden beams and exposed stone walls, is lightly furnished with leather sofas, leafy plants and wood-burning stove; the bedroom is similarly cool and uncluttered, the bathroom flourishes soya candles and a sunken jacuzzi. From balcony and terrace are long valley views to Fowey, peeping over distant hilltops. There are walks from the door, and woodland, orchards and wildlife ponds aplenty… perfect peace. *Children over 12 welcome.*

Price	£570 per week (£95 per night).
Rooms	Cottage for 2.
Meals	Restaurant 1.5 miles.
Closed	Rarely.
Directions	From r'bout at Four Turnings, take ferry exit signed Passage Lane. 0.5 miles on left, turn for Penventinue & follow Old Watermill B&B signs; after 0.5 miles on left.

Carrie King
Coriander Cottages: Badger's Hollow,
The Old Watermill, Penventinue Lane,
Fowey, Cornwall PL23 1JT

Tel	+44 (0)1726 834998
Email	carrie@coriandercottages.co.uk
Web	www.coriandercottages.co.uk

Ethical Collection: Environment.
See page 211.

Price band: C

Red & Blue Houses & The Yurt at Adventure Cornwall

In a corner of a Cornish orchard is a domed Mongolian yurt. On a floor strewn with colourful rugs are futon mattresses, a table and chairs and a small gas cooker, all contained in a frame made from locally grown steam-bent ash. Outside are a hammock, chairs and barbecue. By day, light streams in from a circular vent; at night, stoke up the wood-burner and light the candle lanterns. A five-minute walk through tall grasses brings you to cooking facilities, loos, solar-powered showers and WiFi. As for the newly converted farm buildings, they are beautiful, bright and modern inside. Expect high ceilings, exposed beams, big sofas, wood-burning stoves – and a covered 'link' with a long pine table, perfect for big parties. Each has underfloor heating, rainwater tanks and composting loos, solar panels and renewable tariffs; two wind turbines are on their way. There's masses of outdoor space, massages to order, even a wood-fired hot tub to soak in. For the adventurous: a climbing wall, an archery net and canoe trips (led by David) down the Fowey river. Fabulous. *5% refund & free recharging for electric cars.*

Price	£320–£1,520. Yurt £320–£750. Prices per week.
Rooms	Blue House & Red House sleep 6 each. The Yurt sleeps 5 (separate shower block).
Meals	Restaurants/pub walking distance.
Closed	The Yurt: November–March.
Directions	A38 for Plymouth; at Dobwalls, A390 signed St Austell. Thro' East Taphouse, B3359 for 4 miles; right for Polruan, thro' Lanteglos Highway; right to Mixtow, right at T-junc. On left.

Ethical Collection: Environment.
See page 211.

Price band: C

David & Catherine Collin
Adventure Cornwall,
Lombard Farm, Mixtow,
Fowey, Cornwall PL23 1NA

Tel	+44 (0)1726 870844
Email	david@adventurecornwall.co.uk
Web	www.adventurecornwall.co.uk

Bedknobs B&B

At first glance, a classic British B&B – but under the pale green décor lies a seam of deep green: Gill and husband Kim have restored and refined their Victorian villa with environmental responsibility at the top of the list. From the solar-heated water coursing through the pipes to the perfectly reconstructed Victorian conservatory, their labour has been one of love and loyalty, both to principle and to the period of the house. Rooms are well equipped and adorned with grand Louis XV-style beds; native timbers and non-toxic paints have been used throughout. Gill, a B&B trailblazer, has sourced the greenest products possible for the bathrooms, one of which has an air bath (an air-circulated jacuzzi) so you can come home to a bit of luxury after the rigours of the North Cornwall coast. Each room is named after the particular tree it overlooks – 'Beeches', 'Laurel', 'Yew' – and the garden is a mini-Heligan with its huge bamboo, leggy rhododendrons and ruined hothouse. Bodmin is a five-minute walk, and beyond the town is the moor – Cornwall 'proper'! *Minimum stay two nights at weekends, three nights on bank holidays.*

Price	£75–£95. Discounts for those arriving via public transport.
Rooms	3: 2 doubles; 1 twin/double with separate bath.
Meals	Picnic lunches £5–£10. Wine from £7.50. Restaurants nearby.
Closed	Never.
Directions	Westward on A30, exit for Bodmin, using r/h lane. First right into Castle Street. Pass Love Lane on left, Cross Lane on right. Bedknobs third driveway on left.

Gill Jenkins
Bedknobs B&B,
Polgwyn, Castle Street,
Bodmin, Cornwall PL31 2DX

Tel	+44 (0)1208 77553
Email	gilly@bedknobs.co.uk
Web	www.bedknobs.co.uk

Ethical Collection: Environment. See page 211.

Price band: C

East Penrest Farm

In a fabulous farmyard setting, this stunning stone and slate low-energy barn on the edge of the Tamar Valley is double-insulated with a centrepiece wood-burner using renewable wood from the farm's hedgerows. On the ground floor, where farm animals once munched, guests sleep in a row of cosy beamed, flagged bedrooms, each with a stable door to the south-facing patio. Upstairs, the old threshing barn has been transformed into a breathtaking, convivial space: a light-filled, 50ft-long open-plan living area with a kitchen at one end and a book-filled snug at the other. Easy-going country antiques, rugs on pitch pine floors and old map prints add to the charm — all topped off by the beautifully restored beamed ceiling. Owners Jo and James, who hold charity barn dances and big breakfasts on their 120-acre estate, farm organically and are happy for families to meet the sheep and the cows. Green-fingered Jo can supply home-grown veg and organic lamb, and will rustle up dinner if requested. A charming pub is a walk away; Launceston, the ancient capital of Cornwall, is five miles.

Price	£400–£1,500 per week.
Rooms	House for 8–10.
Meals	Dinner, 2 courses with apple juice, from £12 p.p. Restaurant 750m.
Closed	Never.
Directions	From Exeter A30 to Launceston, then A388 for Plymouth; in Treburley, right at Springer Spaniel pub towards Trebillet; 750 yds on left.

Ethical Collection: Environment;
Community; Food.
See page 211.

Price band: C

Jo & James Rider
East Penrest Farm,
Lezant, Launceston,
Cornwall PL15 9NR

Tel   +44 (0)1579 370186
Email   jrider@lineone.net

Buttervilla Farm

Gill and Robert are so good at growing vegetables – and amazingly flavoursome tomatoes – that they supply the local restaurants, including Jamie Oliver's Fifteen. They're pretty good at looking after you too, in a totally relaxed fashion, delivering award-winning breakfasts of superb rare-breed bacon, and modern Cornish suppers; fish and Red Ruby steak are specialities. A treat to come home to after a long day striding the Cornish coastal path or swimming in the nearby six-foot surf. The farm is certified by the Soil Association and Gill and Robert are members of the Organic Environmental Stewardship Scheme (their vision is to offer 100% home-grown organic food in season and they're not far off their target). There's no sitting room but the bedrooms are colourful, comfortable and cared for; bathrooms are smart with solar-powered showers. Explore these 15 beautiful eco-managed acres and keep your activities local, there's so much to do (just ask Gill and Robert); fold-up bicycles to borrow, too. Young and with soul – organic farming at its trendiest. *The station is a mile away & pick-up is free of charge.*

Price	£85–£105.
Rooms	3 doubles.
Meals	Dinner, 3 courses, £30.
	Light dinners £10. Restaurants 3 miles.
Closed	Rarely.
Directions	Turn by Halfway House at Polbathic for Downderry. House 400 yds up hill from inn, on left; signed before lane.

Gill & Robert Hocking
Buttervilla Farm,
Polbathic, St Germans,
Torpoint, Cornwall PL11 3EY

Tel   +44 (0)1503 230315
Email info@buttervilla.com
Web   www.buttervilla.com

Ethical Collection: Environment; Food.
See page 211.

Price band: C

Spekes House

Infinite views of the sea, delicious water flowing from the spring. The Bedfords are to be commended for their protective approach to a precious resource that seems never-ending. Under the organic gardens of this exceptional place lives a complete rainwater harvesting system; within the well-loved, green-powered cottage, water is conserved throughout. This was the Bedfords' family home for ten years, so there's a sitting room with books, pictures, open fire and deep sofas, a dining room with a grand farmhouse table, and a kitchen big enough for cooks to have helpers. Textiles soften warm beech floors and crisp walls, there are pretty jugs on the dresser, stylish curtains at the windows and house plants in every corner. Off the big, bright, sofa'd landing are four bedrooms under the eaves, softly carpeted and with spectacular views. No sound will disturb you, just the whistling of the wind on wild nights. You're up with the elements here and, like a thirst-quenching glass of water, it is wonderfully re-energising – a magical place for writers, artists, walkers, beachcombers and (competent) surfers.

Ethical Collection: Environment.
See page 211.

Price band: C

Price	£750–£2,500 per week.
Rooms	House for 9 (3 doubles, 1 bunkbed room plus single bed; 2 bathrooms).
Meals	Restaurants 3 miles.
Closed	Never.
Directions	Off A39 dir. Hartland; thro' Hartland to Stoke. Sharp left immed. before red phone box signed Elmscott. 0.75 miles; right, signed Elmscott. 0.75 miles to x'roads. Straight over, signed Kernstone. Continue to end of lane. Left-hand gate opens to driveway.

Rupert Bedford
Spekes House,
Spekes Mill Mouth, Hartland,
Bideford, Devon EX39 6DY

Tel	+44 (0)1458 441850
Email	info@spekeshouse.co.uk
Web	www.spekeshouse.co.uk

Burgh Island

Fancy a taste of the Roaring Twenties? Burgh is unique, "green with nail varnish" –
glamorous English Art Deco trapped in aspic. Noel Coward loved it, Agatha Christie
wrote here, now it's a member of the eco revolution for 21st-century dreamers. It's
much more than a hotel: you come to join a cast of players. So sip vermouth in Poirot's
domed Peacock Bar, then swan off to the ballroom and dine on devilishly decadent food
(glistening veg fresh from the hotel's 12-acre organic garden) while the sounds of swing
and jazz fill the air. Don't expect any eco preach (that's not very Art Deco, darling) but
flowers in vases four-feet high, bronze ladies thrusting globes into the sky, walls clad in
vitrolite, and a superb 14th-century smugglers inn serving Burgh Island organic cider.
Art Deco bedrooms are the real thing: Bakelite telephones, ancient radios, panelled
walls. Some have claw-foot baths, others have balconies, all have Belu bottled water, and
the Beach House suite juts out over rocks. You're on an island; either cross the sands at
low tide or hitch a ride on the sea tractor.

Price	Half-board £360–£385. Suites £440–£600.
Rooms	25: 10 doubles, 3 twins/doubles, 12 suites.
Meals	Half-board only. Lunch £38. Dinner for non-residents, 3 courses, £55. Wine from £17.50.
Closed	Rarely.
Directions	Drive to Bigbury-on-Sea. At high tide you are transported by sea tractor, at low tide by Landrover. Walking takes 3 minutes.

Deborah Clark & Tony Orchard
Burgh Island,
Bigbury-on-Sea,
Devon TQ7 4BG

Tel	+44 (0)1548 810514
Email	reception@burghisland.com
Web	www.burghisland.com

Ethical Collection: Food.
See page 211.

Price band: F

Higher Wiscombe

Higher Wiscombe is something of a green beacon for the south west, encouraging all who meet Lorna and Alistair to switch on to sustainability. Young green oak meets ancient beams and timbers, and big windows have panoramic views; you are surrounded by 52 acres of rich chemical-free farmland and wildlife. Cream painted furniture, bright woollen blankets, and huggable stacks of towels in super-duper bathrooms create a contemporary feel. For family gatherings and friends' reunions, choose the Old Winery with its two kitchens (range cookers, slate floors, granite worktops, white china), large sitting room with wood-burner, dining room with oak table that seats 32, and catering for the asking: a professional chef will produce organic feasts. Thatched Barn and Flint Barn are smaller, with range cookers, blue squashy sofas, books and cosy wood-burners. All three have private patio areas with stunning views, while the central courtyard, games room, and heat-exchange-pump-heated outdoor pool (separate time slots for separate parties) are shared. Tumble four miles down deep Devon lanes to the sea.

Price	Flint Barn: £425–£1,595. Thatched Barn: £495–£1,795. Old Winery: £2,250–£5,450. Prices per week.
Rooms	Flint Barn & Thatched Barn sleep 6. Old Winery sleeps 20.
Meals	Dinner with drinks, £15. Restaurant 4 miles.
Closed	Never.
Directions	Directions on booking.

Ethical Collection: Environment; Community. See page 211.

Price band: D

Lorna Handyside
Higher Wiscombe,
Southleigh, Colyton,
Devon EX24 6JF

Tel	+44 (0)1404 871360
Email	alistair@higherwiscombe.com
Web	www.higherwiscombe.com

Upcott House

Upcott is an Arts and Crafts gem – a big rambling house with its own little turret, revived by Liz and Malcolm in an eco-friendly way. Local stone and timbers were sought out, carpets were pulled up to reveal original boards, harsh strip lighting made way for discreet spot lighting – and the odd glistening chandelier – rough walls were made smooth and eco-tinted in subtle colours, and everything that could be reused has been. Stained-glass windows and period detail rub shoulders with slick leather sofas, funky fabrics and contemporary pieces. The spacious living room has a wood-burning stove; the kitchen has sleek units armed with every conceivable utensil – and you can help yourself to vegetables from the greenhouse. Upstairs, bedrooms have chunky wooden beds with sumptuous mattresses; one has a balcony, another the turret, all have blissful views. More gorgeous things to gawp at in the super bathrooms, where hot water is generated from solar panels hidden in the roof slates. Lawns slope to the garden's edge and the sparkling blue sea sweeps beyond. *Organic hamper on arrival. Minimum stay two nights.*

Price	£1,950–£3,500 per week.
Rooms	House for 12 + cots (4 doubles, 2 twins).
Meals	Restaurant 0.3 miles.
Closed	Never.
Directions	Head for B3174 Beer Road (linking Seaton & Beer). Turn onto Old Beer Road with sea on right. Upcott is just before road narrows to single file.

Liz & Malcolm Robinson
Upcott House,
Old Beer Road, Seaton,
Beer, Devon EX12 2PZ
Tel   +44 (0)1297 20307
Email   enquiries@devonretreat.com
Web   www.devonretreat.com

Ethical Collection: Environment; Food.
See page 211.

Price band: C

Entry 14   Map 1

The Sea House

Sheltered by a shingle bank, 12 paces from the sea, is an inspired renovation of a ferryman's cottage. Natural materials (limestone, travertine, limewashed panelling) combine with deceptively simple touches (hand-turned walnut knobs, gingham curtains, handmade quilts) to create warm and harmonious interiors. A large area of decking overlooks the ever-changing views of river and sea, so you can watch the yachts and small fishing boats chug in and out of harbour. The sunny character of the rooms reflects Pepita's personality and the overall impression is one of creativity, generosity and space. Water is solar-powered, heating is from renewable sources, food, treats and toiletries are local, cycle and bus routes are provided. And windows open inwards so there's no rattling in stormy weather – a thoughtful touch, considering winds reach 100mph in winter! As the coffee warms on the stove and you plan the day's adventures – a trip to Lyme Regis, a stroll to Seaton to stock up the larder – you'll feel happy to be here, in blissful comfort on the edge of the sea.

Price	£80–£150. Whole house (sleeps 6) £1,500 per week.
Rooms	3 twins/doubles. House available for self-catering.
Meals	Dinner £25. Wine £25. Restaurant within walking distance.
Closed	Rarely.
Directions	From A35 coastal road, A358 for Seaton. B3172 to Axmouth. Through village to Harbour Road. Or, by train to Axminster, bus to Seaton stop Axmouth Harbour. Walk past the chandlers.

Ethical Collection: Environment.
See page 211.

Price band: E

Pepita Collins
The Sea House,
2 Harbour Cottage, Axmouth,
Seaton, Devon EX12 4AB

Tel	+44 (0)1297 22650
Email	harbourdetail@btinternet.com
Web	www.harbourdetail.com

The Mill at Gordleton

A 400-year-old listed mill; plans are afoot to reactivate the old wheel in order to draw electricity from it. The low-energy house sits in two acres of English country garden with Avon water tumbling over the weir; mallards, lampreys, Indian runners and leaping trout all call it home. It's an idyllic spot, the terrace perfect for summer suppers with the stream brushing past below. Inside, low ceilings, warm colours and wonky walls give the feel of cottage life. A fire roars in reception, a panelled bar serves pre-dinner drinks. Colourful bedrooms are full of character; one is directly above the wheel house and comes with mind-your-head beams. Expect check fabrics, furry throws, sheets and blankets, bowls of fruit. Three rooms have watery views (you can fall asleep to the sound of the river), two have small sitting rooms, and while a lane passes outside, you are more likely to be woken by birdsong. Downstairs, the restaurant offers delicious locally sourced food: confit of duck, loin of pork and an irresistible banana soufflé. The coast is close. *Coiled-piped heat exchange in the river supplies 80% of energy.*

Price	£130–£150. Suites £150–£210.
Rooms	7: 1 double, 4 twins/doubles, 2 suites.
Meals	Lunch from £8.95. Dinner, 3 courses, about £35. Wine from £14.95.
Closed	Christmas Day.
Directions	South from Brockenhurst on A337. Under railway bridge, over roundabout & 1st right, signed Hordle. On right after 2 miles.

Liz Cottingham
The Mill at Gordleton,
Silver Street, Hordle, Lymington,
Hampshire SO41 6DJ

Tel +44 (0)1590 682219
Email info@themillatgordleton.co.uk
Web www.themillatgordleton.co.uk

Ethical Collection: Environment; Food.
See page 211.

Price band: E

Woodsmans Loft

Slip off your shoes (please!) and step in to a wool-carpeted, eco-insulated, light-filled bolthole for two. Three miles from Jane Austen's house at Chawton, in lovely leafy Hampshire, is an exemplary loft conversion of a spanking new garage. Builder and green pioneer Jo set up a building consultancy before sustainability became trendy, and her handsome new-builds follow a classical style. Cosily under the eaves, this open-plan space is as cleverly designed as can be. The roof harvests rain for the garden, the insulation is Ecotherm, the towels are bamboo fibre, the cotton is organic, the teas are fairtrade – and the patio sandstone comes from ethically run quarries. Walls and sloping ceilings are creamy white, Jane Churchill fabrics add texture and pizazz: a deep-red bedspread, a big-spot kitchen blind. Behind are the woods so you wake to the birds, opposite is a field filled with Friesians in summer, beyond are the family's rescue ponies. Stock up in Alton for farmers' market goodies – and if you tire of your well-equipped corner kitchen, the good pub is a stroll. *Minimum stay two nights at weekends.*

Price	£60 per night.
Rooms	Studio for 2-4 (1 double, 1 sofabed; 1 bathroom).
Meals	Restaurant 0.75 miles.
Closed	Rarely.
Directions	Onto Froyle Road at Golden Pot pub from B3349 Odiham-Alton. Southfield is at bottom of 1st track on your right, 300 yds up road.

Ethical Collection: Environment; Food.
See page 211.

Price band: C

Jo Lewis
Woodsmans Loft, Southfield House,
Froyle Road, Golden Pot, Alton,
Hampshire GU34 4DA

Tel	+44 (0)1420 87530
Email	southfield.house@btinternet.com
Web	www.woodsmansloft.com

The Coach House, Beech Hill Farm

An unusual set-up – refreshingly so. On her organic smallholding Julia has created a delightful escape for those who come to write, read or paint. The Coach House – oceans of daffodils to one side, quiet country road to the other – has been designed as an open-plan, ground-floor retreat. The living area, rising to its 200-year-old rafters, has contemporary Scandinavian-style furniture, bold splashes of colour, and kilims on a sweep of maple parquet that runs from the sitting room and through folding doors to the bedroom on the other side. The streamlined kitchen is also here, neatly tucked under the dormer and excellently equipped. Soothing to look out across the wild garden to the beauty of the High Weald as you rustle up a meal (home-grown mutton, maybe?). The fabrics are natural, the water (for main house) solar, the sheep (Wensleydale) rare-breed, and Julia runs knitting courses using their wool. Extra guests or friends can stay in the main house – or the Studio, a flexible project space. Gardens, Glyndebourne and a really good food pub are a mile away. *Award-winning rainwater harvesting system.*

Price	3 nights £225 (£325-£450 per week).
Rooms	House for 2-3 (1 twin/double; folding bed).
Meals	Restaurants 1 mile.
Closed	Rarely.
Directions	A267 to Heathfield; B2096 to Battle. Right at Chapel Cross to Rushlake Green, through village to Cowbeech & Hailsham. 1 mile on left, opposite Oast. White verge posts.

	Julia Desch The Coach House, Beech Hill Farm, Rushlake Green, Heathfield, Sussex TN21 9QB
Tel	+44 (0)1435 830203
Email	julia@desch.go-plus.net
Web	www.sussexcountryretreat.co.uk

Ethical Collection: Environment; Community. See page 211.

Price band: C

Rye Bay Beach House

The sun's energy is captured by solar tubes, the eco roof system blends into the landscape and the shared wind turbines generate power. This is a new development that combines sustainability with style, delightful for a family small or large, and the garden room den off the garage makes a great bolthole for teens. There are curved 'turrets' and cedar shingles, patio glass doors onto balconies and communal spaces where palms will soon mature. A small but well-equipped kitchen – the Dualit toaster sets the tone – lies off a living room furnished in retro-70s fashion (gleaming wooden floor, vintage pieces, white walls) while the iPod deck is entirely contemporary. As are the bedrooms with their white metal bedframes on carpeted floors and low-energy lamps on tables. Off the double is a big decked balcony with views to the dunes: Camber's glory. The summer crowds flock to this rare stretch of unshingle beach, and when the tide is out you can walk half a mile to the waves – or hitch a ride on a donkey. Five minutes away is Rye with a farmers' market on Wednesdays, and some of the loveliest streets in the country.

Price	£425–£696 per week.
Rooms	House for 4-6 (1 double, 1 twin; sofabed in den).
Meals	Restaurant nearby.
Closed	Rarely.
Directions	M20 junc. 10 for A2070 (Brenzett). Straight on for 9 miles dir. Rye (A259); after 6 miles, left for Camber; after 2.5 miles, right on Old Lydd Rd.

Ethical Collection: Environment.
See page 211.

Price band: C

Marcie Gatsky
Rye Bay Beach House,
Royal William Square,
Camber, Sussex TN31 7RX

Mobile	+44 (0)7961 377365
Email	ryebaybeachhouse@gmail.com
Web	www.ryebaybeachhouse.com

Entry 19   Map 1

The True Heart

Come for locally sourced full English: Gloucester sausages and bacon, farmhouse free-range eggs and home-grown tomatoes, served in the flower-lined front garden. Or in the cosy bohemian dining room, a friendly mix of modern and antique. Come, too, for the pastel bathrooms with their natural soaps (old soaps are recycled by local homeless shelter), soft organic cotton towels and solar-heated showers. Inviting, too, are the pure cotton sheets in the south-facing bedrooms, their bamboo patterns papering well-insulated walls. And come for your vivacious hostess Veronica, with her joyful approach to life and her down-to-earth green vision. As for Frampton on Severn, it's an English delight, with its 16th-century manor house in 1,500 acres, its gentle river walks and immense village green, its tea shops and old-fashioned pubs serving large lunches. A pretty, late-Georgian cottage (and a pub until the 60s!), The True Heart is aptly named: heart-warming B&B links arms with sustainability and sincerity. Leave the petrol-guzzler at home: Frampton is too pretty to be clogged with cars. *Children over 12 welcome.*

Price	£85. Singles £55.
Rooms	3: 1 double en suite; 1 double, 1 twin sharing bath.
Meals	Restaurants within walking distance.
Closed	Never.
Directions	From M5 exit 13, A38 for Bristol; 2nd right almost opp. Texaco garage. 1st left thro' village green; entrance 0.6 miles on right, before turn to Vicarage Lane.

Veronica Metcalfe
The True Heart,
The Street, Frampton on Severn,
Gloucestershire GL2 7ED

Tel	+44 (0)1452 740504
Email	veronica@thetrueheart.co.uk
Web	www.thetrueheart.co.uk

Ethical Collection: Environment;
Community; Food.
See page 211.

Price band: C

Entry 20   Map 1

The Peren

Herons, kingfishers, badgers… they'll all find their way to your private wildflower meadow. In front is The Peren, past the part-canopied terrace with table, chairs and barbecue. In this superb, stylish conversion of a mid-Victorian barn, handsome double-height windows replace the vast threshing door. The sofa demands you curl up in front of the wood-burner and a welcome hamper of local produce sits temptingly on the little antique kitchen table. Up an open-plan staircase to oak floors (FSC certified) and a bed that peers out through a huge window. There's an exciting glass walkway to the spotless family bathroom with stone floors and a double-ended bath (greener to share!). Children have space to run and a toy box to explore. Simon and Andrew did a stint in London and moved here for the green life: The Peren has energy conservation at its heart, with geothermal underfloor heating and low-energy lighting just the start. They have an organic smallholding nearby (collect your breakfast eggs) where the local community can help to rear organic pork. Hay-on-Wye is a short, flat cycle ride away. Delightful.

Price	£350–£850 per week.
Rooms	House for 5 (1 double, 1 triple; 1 bath, 1 shower).
Meals	Restaurant 2 miles.
Closed	Rarely.
Directions	1.5 miles from Hay on B4350, turn left as you enter Clifford in front of cream house. Next right, down tree-tunnelled lane. The Peren is 500 yds on left.

Ethical Collection: Environment; Community; Food.
See page 211.

Price band: C

Simon Forrester & Andrew Craven
The Peren,
Lower Wyeside, Clifford, Hereford,
Herefordshire HR3 5EU

Tel	+44 (0)1497 831225
Email	info@theperen.com
Web	www.theperen.com

Ecocabin

If you were dreaming of building an eco home you might want to model it on Kate's remarkable and oh-so-natural achievement. Everything here is as sustainable as can be, and funky and comfortable too. Outside, it looks like a vast, interesting garden shed. Within, there is an unassuming naturalness: floors of ash, walls clay-painted and lime-plastered. Splashes of colour (bright red sofas and armchairs, chunky blue checks on bedcovers) set off the whiteness and wood. Tiles are hand-made, simple and eye-catching. The wood-pellet stove is a feature, with a reclaimed-slate surround. All the fabrics are natural: organic cotton towels and bedding, and naturally dyed curtains. Soaps for washing and cleaning are earth-friendly; recycled furniture comes from a local community scheme. And to top it all off, this is a lush part of England four miles from Clun; you will see curlew and buzzard, wild flowers aplenty and fruits to pick from the hedges. Wild flowers strew the garden, too; there are log 'planters' and a barbecue from a local blacksmith. Unforgettable. *5% discount if you leave the car at home.*

Price	£85–£105 (£378–£605 per week).	
Rooms	Cabin for 4 (1 double, 1 twin; bath/shower).	
Meals	Shopping service provided. Restaurant 5 miles.	
Closed	Never.	
Directions	From Hopton Heath, take turn for Hopton Castle; at Obley Chapel T-junc., left, then immed right. Ecocabin on left.	

Kate Grubb
Ecocabin,
Obley, Bucknell,
Shropshire SY7 0BY
Tel   +44 (0)1547 530183
Email   kate@ecocabin.co.uk
Web   www.ecocabin.co.uk

Ethical Collection: Environment; Food. See page 211.

Price band: D

Entry 22   Map 1

Carrick's at Castle Farm

A comfortable, and jolly, mix of farmhouse and B&B — tractors and rare-breed cattle, and a large warm-bricked house of local red with a rather swish interior and a home-quarried floor. Both Jean and John are passionate about biodiversity and conservation and here you have absolute quiet for birdwatching, fishing or walking; recover in the drawing room with its books and river views from long windows. Walls are warmly wrapped to keep in the heat provided by a biomass boiler. Bedrooms are large, light and well-thought-out with great bathrooms and binoculars. Food is home-grown or local: they have a farm shop for tasty souvenirs, and there's always coffee and cake, or wine, on arrival; the hospitality here is outstanding. The pretty garden leads down to the river Wensum and a footpath. The farm is part of DEFRA's Higher Level Stewardship Scheme: species-rich grasslands are carefully managed and soil is protected. There are skylark plots, lapwing nesting and specially created habitats for winter wading birds. Green points scored for their inspirational conservation work.

Price	From £75. Singles £55.
Rooms	4: 2 doubles en suite; 1 double, 1 twin each with separate bath (let to same party only).
Meals	Dinner, 3 courses, £20. BYO. Pub 0.5 miles.
Closed	Never.
Directions	From Norwich A47 to Dereham (don't go into Dereham). B1147 to Swanton Morley. In village, take Elsing Road at Darby's pub; farm drive 0.5 miles on left.

Ethical Collection: Environment;
Community; Food.
See page 211.

Price band: C

Jean Wright
Carrick's at Castle Farm,
Castle Farm, Swanton Morley,
Dereham, Norfolk NR20 4JT

Tel	+44 (0)1362 638302
Email	jean@castlefarm-swanton.co.uk
Web	www.carricksatcastlefarm.co.uk

Strattons

I had a dream and it was Strattons. It tops the polls for the greenest hotel in the UK and every square inch of the delightful Queen Anne villa has been rigorously researched to be kinder to the environment. But what is truly special is Les and Vanessa's enviro-artistic style: the shimmering mermaid mosaic pieced together from broken china; the reincarnation of wine bottle bottoms in the patio terrace; the resplendent sculptured stag – a symbol of The Brecks – from recycled agricultural iron. Then there are the silky bantams strutting on the lawn and the funky classical interiors with their marble busts, cow-hide rugs on stripped wood floors and art packed tight on the walls – Vanessa and Les actively encourage local artists. Strattons is an informal bohemian country-house bolthole of French inspiration; bedrooms are exquisite and individual: a carved four-poster, a tented bathroom. Food in the candlelit restaurant is delicious and mostly organic, perhaps slow-cooked leg of Papworth lamb followed by rhubarb and ginger crème brûlée; breakfast is equally fine. Superb sustainable style.

Price	£150–£175. Singles from £120. Suites from £200.
Rooms	10: 1 twin/double, 4 doubles, 5 suites.
Meals	Dinner, 4 courses, £40. Wine from £15.
Closed	One week at Christmas.
Directions	Ash Close runs off north end of market place between W H Brown estate agents & fish & chip restaurant.

Vanessa & Les Scott
Strattons,
4 Ash Close, Swaffham,
Norfolk PE37 7NH

Tel +44 (0)1760 723845
Email enquiries@strattonshotel.com
Web www.strattonshotel.com

Ethical Collection: Environment; Community; Food.
See page 211.

Price band: E

Entry 24 Map 1

Church Farm Cottage, Church Farm

You can give a helping hand at lambing or harvest time... animal lovers, environmentalists and children should love this place. The cottage originally formed part of the listed farmhouse; the family have farmed here since time immemorial and one building is listed in the Domesday Book. Managed organically, the summer meadows brim with wild flowers and herbs, while the farmyard could be Old MacDonald's: dogs, cats, hens, cows roam, sheep have their own names. Sue's touch extends inside to the shining copper and brass, the fresh flowers and the examples of her own stencilling and embroidery. A red sofa and chairs cosy up to the original (but super-efficient) range, and all water is solar-heated. Floral curtains, iron latches on kitchen cupboard doors and a traditional white china sink add to the cottagey mood. The attic twin has delightful yellow toile de Jouy bedheads and matching curtains. Add a small, secure cottage garden and dreamy views and you have a rural idyll. There are three more special cottages in the grounds if this one is booked. *Pets by arrangement.*

Price	£392-£674 per week.
Rooms	Cottage for 4 (1 double, 1 twin; 1 bath, 1 shower).
Meals	Restaurant 2 miles.
Closed	Never.
Directions	M1 exit 25; A515 to Ashbourne & Buxton. Left opposite Newton Chalets, left at river, through Milldale & up valley to Watt Russel pub; left then 1st left to Stanshope & left immediately after hall.

Ethical Collection: Environment; Food. See page 211.

Price band: B

Mrs Sue Fowler
Church Farm Cottage,
Church Farm, Stanshope, Alstonefield,
Ashbourne, Derbyshire DE6 2AD
Tel +44 (0)1335 310243
Email sue@dovedalecottages.fsnet.co.uk
Web www.dovedalecottages.co.uk

Entry 25   Map 1

Tyas Cottage

Not easy to find, but what a discovery – a stunningly restored old weaver's cottage cum barn. Old mills, drystone walls, sheep-dotted hills: this dramatic north Pennine landscape deserves to be better known. Here, local materials and modern comforts combine: the huge queen truss in the living room comes from a nearby mill, the carved chimney lintel is original, colourful rugs dot toasty flagged floors (heated underfoot by a heat pump) and Cape Dutch antiques and contemporary Chilean rushback chairs add style. The large open-plan kitchen has every mod con; the dramatic living room is up a metal spiral stair. A glorious Georgian four-poster dominates the master bedroom with its wooded valley views; hot water in the en suite bathrooms is generated from solar panels. You get your own paved entrance and enclosed stepped garden while the shared gardens beyond, bounded by a small mill pond and stream, are astonishing (Victoria is a landscape architect) and include two sculpted swings. Birds abound – herons, kingfishers, owls. From the tap comes fresh spring water for delicious tea. *Minimum stay three nights.*

Price	£360-£500 per week for 2. Extra person £15 per night.
Rooms	Cottage for 6 (1 double, 2 twins, 2 baths; 1 shower).
Meals	Restaurant 0.75 miles.
Closed	Never.
Directions	M62 junc. 24, signs to Rochdale at r'bout. Cross M62; 2nd left signed Pole Moor; 2nd right (Laund Road), until sign 'Road Ahead Impassable'. Before you reach it, turn left down Tyas Lane. Before bottom of hill, cottage to left of cobbled lane.

Victoria Berryman
Tyas Cottage,
Merrydale, Slaithwaite,
Huddersfield, Yorkshire HD7 5UZ

Tel   +44 (0)1484 841010
Email   vicky.berryman@gmail.com
Web   www.yorkshire-holiday.co.uk

Ethical Collection: Environment.
See page 211.

Price band: C

The Austwick Traddock

Unpretentious and full of traditional comforts, this family-run hotel is a friendly base for walkers – and the Three Peaks are at the door. The house is Georgian with Victorian additions, its name originating from horse sales that took place in next door's paddock. Open fires smoulder on winter days, deckchairs dot the garden in summer and country-house bedrooms have bags of charm: antique dressing tables, quilted beds, perhaps a claw-foot bath. Those on the second floor have a cosy attic feel, all have fresh fruit, flat-screen TVs, homemade shortbread and Dales views. It's not yet wildly eco but you will eat in the first hotel restaurant in the north of England to be certified 100% Soil Association organic, so dig into seared scallops, wild venison, lemon soufflé with a Yorkshire curd sorbet. There's a cheerful William Morris feel to it all – polished brass in front of the fire, a panelled breakfast room – while the village, with two clapper bridges, is a gem. If you're around for a local event, feast on the hotel's organic hog roast and raise money for the local community centre and playing fields.

Ethical Collection: Community; Food.
See page 211.

Price band: E

Price	£140–£185. Singles £80–£110. Half-board from £85 p.p.
Rooms	11: 8 doubles, 1 twin/double, 1 family, 1 single.
Meals	Lunch £13–£20. Dinner, 3 courses, about £35. Wine from £15.
Closed	Rarely.
Directions	0.75 miles off the A65, midway between Kirkby Lonsdale & Skipton, 4 miles north-west of Settle.

Bruce Reynolds
The Austwick Traddock,
Austwick, Settle,
Yorkshire LA2 8BY

Tel	+44 (0)1524 251224
Email	info@austwicktraddock.co.uk
Web	www.austwicktraddock.co.uk

Natural Retreats, Yorkshire Dales

Tucked into a wooded hillside, these brand new single-storey, luxury eco residences provide a glimpse of the future. Timber from sustainable woodland provides the support, grass grows long over the sloping roofs, and there's recycled paper for thick insulation. Each little house has its own wormery and some have composting toilets. There are biomass heaters, water harvesters, and ground-source pumps. An organic hamper welcomes new arrivals, there's a natural spring to fill the bath, and a cosy log stove to keep you warm long into the evening. The huge flat-screen TV (powered by renewables) and leather sofa exemplify contemporary living, so too does the well-equipped, über-cool kitchen with matching crockery and microwave. Daylight floods in through the south-facing, floor-to-ceiling, solar-glazed windows revealing the magnificent view of the Swale Valley where rabbits play and red deer can sometimes be seen darting between the trees. And the glorious Yorkshire Dales are on your doorstep. Inspirational. *Percentage of profits supports local sustainable & eco-friendly schemes.*

Price	£770–£1,210 per week.
Rooms	18 houses for 6 (2 doubles, 1 twin/double).
Meals	Restaurant 1 mile.
Closed	Never.
Directions	1 mile from Richmond; 5 miles from A1. From Darlington train station, bus to Richmond; taxi or walk for 1 mile.

Louisa Bexon & Ewan Kearney
Natural Retreats,
Units 1-3, Aislabeck Plantation,
Hurgill Road, Richmond, Yorkshire DL10 4SG

Tel	+44 (0)161 2422970
Email	info@naturalretreats.com
Web	www.naturalretreats.com

Ethical Collection: Environment; Community. See page 211.

Price band: C

Boot & Shoe Cottage

Pure *Wind in the Willows*. The waters of the River Tees pass the bottom of your garden – hire a rod and fish for trout. The 300-year-old cottage was once a cobbler's home, hence its name; the Peats found leather lasts during the renovation. All is simple and immaculate within, a beautiful reincarnation of local reclaim. A fireplace built of stone is the focal point of the comfy sitting room, where pale shades and crisp white woodwork blend with country antiques. The kitchen is compact; its dining end has a table by the wood-burner and French windows open onto the terrace with roses, barbecue and steps to the river. Sunshine streams through the window of the cream-walled double bedroom with its ancient wooden headboard and cast-iron fire; under the rafters is a fun little eyrie for two. You are two miles from an excellent farm shop so rustle up a picnic and walk the glorious Teesdale Way – or loll by the river with its kingfishers, moorhens and ducks. Rachel has planted thousands of trees that enhance the ancient oaks – admire them on route to tennis. *Adjoining twin bedroom also available.*

Price	£290–£435 per week.
Rooms	Cottage for 4 (1 double, 1 twin; 1 bathroom).
Meals	Restaurant 1 mile.
Closed	Never.
Directions	3 miles north of A66 take Greta Bridge turn-off. In Wycliffe village continue on to the Private Road, following the river upstream for 300 yds.

Ethical Collection: Environment; Food. See page 211.

Price band: B

	Mrs Rachel Peat Boot & Shoe Cottage, Wycliffe, Barnard Castle, Durham DL12 9TR
Tel	+44 (0)1833 627200
Email	info@bootandshoecottage.co.uk
Web	www.bootandshoecottage.co.uk

Augill Castle

Built 180 years ago for an eccentric solicitor, this Victorian gentleman's fantasy has become a wildly grand yet intimate green retreat. One of Simon and Wendy's passions is slow living, so recycled finds mix with antiques, open fires crackle with estate logs, veg comes from the kitchen garden, and hens are fed on kitchen waste. Bedrooms are historic but homely, old rugs warm polished floors, there are homemade biscuits and eco-weave (quick-drying) dressing gowns, no timetables and an unrushed staff. Heating and water systems run on LPG (cleaner and more efficient than oil), stoves and open fires are fuelled with naturally felled timber from managed local forests, toiletries are hand-made from organic ingredients, lights are low energy, and they have reduced their rubbish output by 50% over 12 months. Simon and Wendy also run Little Augill Cooks, which aims to introduce children to the fun of cooking real food, sponsor local sports clubs and sell teddies to help fund a local charity. Dinners are convivial... a treat for all ages.

Price	£160. Singles £80.
Rooms	12: 6 doubles, 3 twins/doubles, 3 four-posters.
Meals	Dinner, 4 courses, £40 (Fridays & Saturdays). Midweek supper, 2 courses, £20 by arrangement in winter only. Wine £16–£80.
Closed	Never.
Directions	M6 junc. 38; A685 through Kirkby Stephen. Just before Brough, right for South Stainmore; signed on left after 1 mile.

	Simon & Wendy Bennett Augill Castle, Brough, Kirkby Stephen, Cumbria CA17 4DE
Tel	+44 (0)1768 341937
Email	enquiries@stayinacastle.com
Web	www.stayinacastle.com

Ethical Collection: Environment; Community; Food. See page 211.

Price band: E

Southlands Farm: East Cottage, West Cottage and Middle Cottage

Easy to fall in love with this rugged county for its beauty and its space; no crowds, no traffic jams, no hurry. Stay in a 19th-century byre and granary, beautifully and sustainably converted by owners Charles and Dee. Solar panels heat as much water as possible, electricity comes from renewable sources, the logs are on the house. Walk straight in to a light, modern home; each cottage is lovely. East Cottage has soaring ceilings, ceramic tiles warm underfoot, bright rugs and cushions, a wood-burning stove; the kitchen glows at the other end with hand-built Shaker-style units, granite tops, an old pine dresser with plenty of china, and a good table for long lazy breakfasts. Up the spiral stairs are immaculate bedrooms with buttermilk walls, wooden floors and pastel-striped blankets on exquisite beds. A 20-minute walk brings you to an excellent pub, but have a sundowner on your patio first. Or stay put and choose a delicious supper from the honesty freezer. And if you choose to go B&B, Dee will deliver a sizzling full English breakfast, local and organic. *Middle Cottage links with East Cottage.*

Price	£300–£800 per week.
	Short breaks from £213. B&B £45 p.p.
Rooms	West Cottage for 4. East Cottage for 4.
	Middle Cottage for 2.
Meals	B&B option. Restaurant 0.6 miles.
Closed	Never.
Directions	From Hexham (A69), right to Acomb, straight over Chollerford x-roads; at Chollerton, left at church for Barrasford. Turn right past village into Gunnerton, then 1st right after phone box.

Ethical Collection: Environment; Food.
See page 211.

Price band: C

Charles & Dee McGowan
Southlands Farm,
Gunnerton, Hexham,
Northumberland NE48 4EA

Tel	+44 (0)1434 681464
Email	charles@southlandsfarmcottages.co.uk
Web	www.southlandsfarmcottages.co.uk

Entry 31   Map 1

Battlesteads Hotel

In the land of castles, stone circles and Hadrian's Wall is an old inn given a fresh lease of life by keen greens Richard and Dee. Today the entire hotel is lit using the same amount of power that was used in the bar and lounge alone, the biomass boiler is supplemented by solar panels, and fuelled by chippings from the local forest. "Once the green bug gets you, you find more and more to include": Richard's commitment is ongoing. Bedrooms are spacious, carpeted and comfortable, the newest, with wheelchair access, on the ground floor. Elsewhere: a large, cosy, low-beamed bar, with logs in the wood-burner and local cask ales on hand pump, and an 80-seat dining room, all leather chairs at dark wood tables, light from tall windows and a sweep of new floor. There's also a sunny conservatory that reaches into a walled garden dotted with bird boxes and feeders. Organic or local? It's a fine balance, but the meat comes from Hexham, the fish from North Shields, the black pudding (delicious!) from up the road, the honey from Nook Farm, the salad leaves are their own. Attentive staff are the icing on the cake.

Price	£95–£120. Singles £55–£95.
Rooms	17: 15 twins/doubles, 2 singles.
Meals	Lunch & dinner from £7.95.
Closed	3 weeks in February.
Directions	From A69 at Hexham, A6079 to Chollerford, then A6320 for Bellingham; Wark is halfway.

Richard & Dee Slade
Battlesteads Hotel,
Wark, Hexham,
Northumberland NE48 3LS

Tel	+44 (0)1434 230209
Email	info@battlesteads.com
Web	www.battlesteads.com

Ethical Collection: Environment; Food.
See page 211.

Price band: D

Entry 32   Map 1

Eshott Hall

Slip into graceful inertia for a weekend, or longer. Ramble and yomp to your heart's content through (some say) the finest countryside in Britain – all dreamy castles and white beaches. You will be indulged in this luxurious listed Palladian house with its heart in the conservation of wildlife and architectural history. Warm bedrooms (biomass heated) promise fine linen, thick fabrics, restful colours; warm bathrooms have large baths and grand views over the estate and its medieval woodland. This is only 20 minutes from Newcastle yet you are surrounded by rare wildlife, thanks to the passionate and proactive work of Ho and Margaret: pipistrelle bats and the enigmatic red squirrel flourish. In the house, stunning architectural features have been meticulously conserved: ceramic floors, working shutters, a rare staircase, a stained-glass window designed by William Morris. The garden is delightful with rare old trees, a Victorian fernery, a covered pergola and oodles of woodland trails. After drinks in the library enjoy local food and organic vegetables from the walled garden – in the candlelit dining room or the reconstructed Lost Wing.

Price	£128–£150. Singles £79–£90.
Rooms	6: 4 doubles, 2 twins/doubles.
Meals	Dinner, 3 courses, £35. Wine from £18. By arrangement. Restaurants 5-minute drive.
Closed	22 December–5 January.
Directions	East off A1, 7 miles north of Morpeth, 9 miles south of Alnwick, at Eshott signpost. Hall gates approx. 1 mile down lane.

Ethical Collection: Environment;
Community; Food.
See page 211.

Price band: E

Ho & Margaret Sanderson
Eshott Hall,
Morpeth,
Northumberland NE65 9EN

Tel	+44 (0)1670 787777
Email	enquiries@eshotthallestate.co.uk
Web	www.eshotthall.co.uk

The Nurtons

After following the gentle meanders of the glorious Wye valley, you will be greeted by Adrian and Elsa. The façade of their history-rich home is Victorian, the interior rambling and intriguing, the site ancient – a flagged area conceals a sacred 'healing bath'. It is refreshing to find an old house practising progressive eco-friendly techniques; your hosts are professional ecologists. Only the gasifying wood-boiler is new; the solar panels adorning an insulated roof were installed by Adrian and Elsa 25 years ago: they have long seen the sense in sustainability. At the back of the house are two basic B&B suites, with private sitting areas inside and out; a double room is in the main part of the house. Bed linen is dried in the open air, toiletries are mostly Ecover. The price reflects the simplicity, the plantsman's garden reflects a passion for all things organic and you breakfast generously – not on bacon and eggs, but on fresh fruits, homebaked bread, delicious muesli, honey from their bees. Tranquil and sincerely green. *Holistic treatments can be booked.*

Price	From £65. Singles from £35.
Rooms	3: 1 double, 1 double & sitting room & child bed, 1 twin & sitting room & sofabed.
Meals	Evening platter £30 (for 2) with glass of wine. Packed lunch £5. Pub 0.75 miles.
Closed	Rarely.
Directions	A466 just north of Tintern village. Drive to house opposite Old Station Tintern.

Adrian & Elsa Wood
The Nurtons,
Tintern,
Monmouthshire NP16 7NX

Tel   +44 (0)1291 689253
Email info@thenurtons.co.uk
Web   www.thenurtons.co.uk

Ethical Collection: Environment; Food.
See page 211.

Price band: C

Mandinam

On a heavenly bluff on the edge of the Beacons, beneath wheeling red kites and moody Welsh skies, lies Mandinam, the 'untouched holy place'. Artistic Marcus and Daniella are its guardians and look after you as friends. Be charmed by bold rugs on wooden floors, weathered antiques, a Finnish wood-burner (fuelled by estate coppice), lofty ceilings, shutters, fires, and scrumptious meals in a red dining room. The simple coach house studio, with hillside terrace and wood-burner, is for dreamers; the elegant four-poster room with heated floors is for sybarites. Watch the sun go down before Daniella's delicious dinner, revel in the peace. Miles of hedgerows and 40,000 trees have been planted in the last five years, creating wildlife havens and replenishing woodland. One of their oak woods has won the gold medal at the Royal Welsh Show and is a certified seed source – grandchildren help with the crop gathering. Beef is produced from traditional breeds (Hereford, Angus, Shorthorn) on a sustainable system; future plans include thatching a listed longhouse using straw from the farm. Wonderful. *Minimum stay two nights.*

Price	£70-£80. Singles by arrangement.
Rooms	2: 1 studio twin/double, 1 four-poster.
Meals	Lunch or picnic from £7.50. Dinner with wine, £25. Restaurants & pubs 2 miles.
Closed	Christmas.
Directions	Left at Llangadog village shop; 50 yds right for Myddfai. Past cemetery, 1st right for Llanddeusant; 1.5 miles, thro' woods on left. Or, by train to Llangadog.

Ethical Collection: Environment; Community; Food.
See page 211.

Price band: C

Daniella & Marcus Lampard
Mandinam,
Llangadog,
Carmarthenshire SA19 9LA

Tel	+44 (0)1550 777368
Email	info@mandinam.co.uk
Web	www.mandinam.co.uk

Mandinam: Shepherd's Hut

Four hundred acres of lovingly conserved green, green grass, valley and Welsh woodland. Veteran oaks of 600 years mark this ancient territory. Life here is totally detached from the frenetic world most of us inhabit and a few days on Mandinam farm slows the speed, allowing a sense of perspective. The Shepherd's Hut plays the part perfectly. Simple, small, warm… noble. Wood coppice fuels the little burner and your tiny stove can heat a hearty stew (ask Daniella, she may make you one of her specials). The soft bed is on stilts so there's space for your things; there's a sink and a little table, too, but eat out by the lake if you can and surrender your soul to the verdant landscape. The Shepherd's Hut is the sustainable master plan of artist and steward of the land, Marcus: your stay here directly helps preserve the beauty around, freeing it from the future tyranny of developers. The hut is on wheels so will leave no trace; the outhouse shower is made from reclaimed materials and is solar-powered and wood-heated, and the compost loo feeds the soil so plants will flourish. A very sweet retreat. *Minimum stay two nights.*

Price	£70–£80 per night.
Rooms	Cabin for 2 (separate shower & wc).
Meals	Dinner from £20, by arrangement (at farmhouse). Restaurants & pubs 2 miles.
Closed	Christmas.
Directions	Left at Llangadog village shop; 50 yds right for Myddfai. Past cemetery, 1st right for Llanddeusant; 1.5 miles, thro' woods on left. Or, by train to Llangadog.

Daniella & Marcus Lampard
Mandinam: Shepherd's Hut,
Llangadog,
Carmarthenshire SA19 9LA

Tel	+44 (0)1550 777368
Email	info@mandinam.co.uk
Web	www.mandinam.co.uk

Ethical Collection: Environment.
See page 211.

Price band: C

Oriel Gwyr

A product designer by trade, John has, quite literally, carved out his first house – in the sought-after hamlet of Rhossili. The project that started as a bachelor-pad dream took years to get the go-ahead, but John's semi-subterranean adventure has finally been realised and is open to all. The challenging planning process in this tightly controlled conservation area demanded John investigate green building techniques, and the results are unusual and impressive. The roof is insulated and grassed over, the odd sun pipe breaks through the turf to funnel daylight down, and there's an air-source heat pump to feed the underfloor heating: you'll like the toasty floors. The whole house is muted, immaculate, curvaceous and double glazed, and John has left his own perfectionist mark: a dining room table crafted from leftover chunks of wood. You are three miles from groceries but a welcome hamper of local and organic food will get you started. The restaurant on the clifftop is a two-minute stroll and it's a short tumble down the path to the sweeping sands of Rhossili beach – one of Wales's finest.

Price	£800-£1,600 per week.
Rooms	House for 8 (3 doubles, 1 twin).
Meals	Restaurant 100 yds.
Closed	Never.
Directions	From Swansea, A4118 to Port Eynon. At Scurlage, right onto B4247 until you reach Rhossili; on right 100m before church.

Ethical Collection: Environment.
See page 211.

Price band: C

John Williams
Oriel Gwyr,
Rhossili,
Swansea SA3 1AU

Tel	+44 (0)1792 391425
Email	orielgwyr@btinternet.com
Web	www.orielgwyr.co.uk

Gliffaes Hotel

A matchless country house – with stonking Welsh sheep's wool insulation – that towers majestically above the river Usk as it pours through the valley below. It is a view to feed the soul, so sit on the stone terrace and drink it in. Pull yourself away and you find 33 acres of compost-fed gardens and woodland that ensure nothing but silence. Bee colonies, a bat nursery and over 2,000 newly planted trees make it a haven for conservation. Interiors, lit mostly by low-energy bulbs, pack a grand punch. Afternoon tea is laid out in a sitting room of panelled walls, shiny wood floors and family portraits, while logs crackle in a magnificent carved fireplace. Fishermen gather in the bar for tall stories then spin through to the restaurant for local, seasonal food (the hotel is part of the Slow Food movement). Elsewhere, country-house bedrooms do the trick. Several have river views, one has a claw-foot bath (heated with the help of an exchanger) overlooking the lawn, all have thick fabrics, wool-lined curtains, antique furniture, a sofa if there's room. Come to cast a fly in the Usk while red kite circle above.

Price	£96-£230. Singles from £88. Half-board from £86 p.p.
Rooms	22: 5 doubles, 13 twins/doubles, 4 singles.
Meals	Light lunches from £5. Dinner, 3 courses, £34. Sunday lunch £18-£24. Wine £3.20.
Closed	January.
Directions	From Crickhowell, A40 west for 2.5 miles. Entrance on left, signed. Hotel 1 mile up winding hill.

James & Susie Suter
Gliffaes Hotel,
Crickhowell,
Powys NP8 1RH

Tel   +44 (0)1874 730371
Email   calls@gliffaeshotel.com
Web   www.gliffaeshotel.com

Ethical Collection: Environment; Food.
See page 211.

Price band: F

Entry 38   Map 1

Penpont

Organic fantastic: the Victorian kitchen gardens are registered with the Soil Association and there's a funky little farm shop from which you can buy the veg. Penpont is lovely: the roofs are slated, the walls a comforting patchwork of old stone, plants and bushes, and Davina and Gavin are the nicest people. The courtyard wing doesn't try to be spectacular, just cosy and human, well-decorated and generous. There's a snug sitting room with a wood-burner – a place for children to escape the adults (or vice-versa) – and a big friendly kitchen: pictures on the walls, a large table and an old dresser, bold checks, lovely colours, and the sight and sound of the rushing river. Bedrooms are simple, attractive, with a familial mix of old furniture, stand-alone basins and plain carpets; water and heating is warmed by the estate's impressive biomass boiler. The river is a great draw: bring a canoe if you have one and spend all day teasing the waters. Behind this great kindly house (with church, dovecot and stables – Grade I-listed) is a handsome old stone bridge leading to walks galore; you feel miles from anywhere.

Price	£1,450–£1,750 per week. Short breaks from £850.
Rooms	Courtyard wing sleeps 15–17 in 6 bedrooms.
Meals	Restaurant 20km.
Closed	Never.
Directions	From Brecon, west on A40 through Llanspyddid. Pass 2nd telephone kiosk on left. Entrance to house on right. Approx. 4.5 miles from Brecon. Sign on right hand side of road.

Ethical Collection: Environment;
Community; Food.
See page 211.

Price band: B

Davina & Gavin Hogg
Penpont,
Brecon,
Powys LD3 8EU
Tel   +44 (0)1874 636202
Email   penpont@btconnect.com
Web   www.penpont.com

The Yat

In a supreme setting of rolling hills studded with sheep is The Yat – proof that a listed house dating from the 15th century can dance to the green beat. Practically everything was reclaimed for restoration; organic wax preserves the floor boards; wool lines the roof. Years ago Krystyna and Derek fell in love with these eight acres, where nature predominates and the only sounds you hear are birdsong and whispering wind. The first thing they did was plant trees on the steep slopes to the sides; now there are 1,000 – mostly deciduous, some coniferous – providing shelter for plants and a wonderful haven for wildlife. The feel of the house, thanks to charming artist Krystyna, is one of calm, and there are many beautiful things to look at, both modern and antique. Bedrooms are quaint, bathrooms simple. Water is seductively heated by solar thermals, paints are non-VOC. Food is almost all organic, breakfasts and suppers scrumptious and local. This is a grand place to rest and recharge; the garden, formal and wild, tiered and fruit-filled, is steeped in history and is complete with a dry-stone-wall restoration project.

Price	£75. Singles from £55.
Rooms	2: 1 double, 1 twin.
Meals	Dinner, 3 courses with wine, £30.
Closed	Rarely.
Directions	Directions from Hundred House village: road to Glascwm, signed at crossroads; at next T-junc., left over humpback bridge; left at next junction; 1st house on right (opp. church).

Krystyna Zaremba
The Yat,
Glascwm, Llandrindod Wells,
Powys LD1 5SE

Tel   +44 (0)1982 570339
Email   krystyna.zaremba@theyat.net
Web   www.theyat.net

Ethical Collection: Environment; Food. See page 211.

Price band: C

Y Goeden Eirin

An education in all things Welsh – culture, food, environment – in a stylish spot from which to explore. Against the backdrop of wild Snowdonia, surrounded by 20 acres of rough grazing, house and setting have an open seaside feel. Inside presents a very cosy picture: Welsh-language and English books share the shelves, paintings by contemporary Welsh artists enliven the walls, an arty 70s décor mingles with sturdy Welsh oak in the bedrooms, and the bathrooms are rather chic. Wonderful locally sourced food is served alongside the (locally renovated) Bechstein in the beamed dining room, eco-friendly soaps are bought in Caernarfon, recycled tissues from Penygroes. Even the electricity is powered by Welsh sunshine thanks to twelve photovoltaic panels (installed with the help of Dyfi Eco park). John and Eluned take care to emphasise an often neglected element of social responsibility, in keeping their heritage, culture and language alive: hear stories from the Mabinogion, learn the history of Welsh place names. The excellent Centre for Alternative Technology is under two hours by bus from Dolydd. Superb all round.

Price	£80–£100. Singles from £60.
Rooms	3: 2 doubles, 1 twin.
Meals	Dinner, 3 courses, £28. Wine from £14. Packed lunch £12. Pub/restaurant 0.75 miles.
Closed	Christmas to New Year & occasionally.
Directions	From Caernarfon onto Porthmadog & Pwllheli road. A487 thro' Bontnewydd, left at r'bout, signed Dolydd. House 0.5 miles on right, last entrance before garage on left.

Ethical Collection: Environment; Food.
See page 211.

Price band: D

Dr John & Mrs Eluned Rowlands
Y Goeden Eirin,
Dolydd, Caernarfon,
Gwynedd LL54 7EF
Tel   +44 (0)1286 830942
Email   john_rowlands@tiscali.co.uk
Web   www.ygoedeneirin.co.uk

Eaglescairnie Mains

Eight acres of conservation headland have been created and 15,000 trees, wild bird cover, new hedges and wildflower meadows planted on this 350-acre working farm... you'd never know Edinburgh was so close. With so many trees being planted (and protected), the Williams family, with the coppiced timber feeding their biomass boiler, are living the sustainable life. Future generations will thank them for it. The Georgian farmhouse sits in lovely gardens, its peace interrupted by the odd strutting pheasant. There's a traditional conservatory for summery breakfasts, a perfectly proportioned drawing room (coral walls, rich fabrics, log fire) for wintery nights, and beautiful big bedrooms full of books. Michael and Barbara are warm and charming, their commitment to the countryside, including involvement in several conservation bodies such as the RSPB, has earned them a range of prestigious awards and the atmosphere is gracious and unhurried. Walk and explore; take a guided tour: if conservation and biodiversity have not caught your imagination before, your head will be full of ideas on your journey home.

Price	£60–£75. Singles from £45.
Rooms	3: 2 doubles, 1 twin.
Meals	Pub 1 mile.
Closed	Christmas.
Directions	From A1 at Haddington, B6368 south for Bolton & Humbie. Right immed. after traffic lights on bridge. 2.5 miles on through Bolton, at top of hill, fork left for Gifford. Entrance 0.5 miles on left.

	Barbara & Michael Williams
	Eaglescairnie Mains,
	Gifford, Haddington,
	East Lothian EH41 4HN
Tel	+44 (0)1620 810491
Email	williams.eagles@btinternet.com
Web	www.eaglescairnie.com

Ethical Collection: Environment; Community. See page 211.

Price band: C

Entry 42   Map 1

Langside Farm

Your hosts are intelligent, humorous and gently working at being squeaky green in their home. Members of the local Slow Food Convivium, keen sourcers of local and fairtrade produce and growers of organic veg, they guarantee you fine breakfasts and lovely Scottish suppers. Chat by the Aga, read by the fire, make yourselves truly at home. Water comes from a private spring, its purity ensured by filtration, and a biomass boiler keeps you cosy; it's fed on forest thinnings from the Blairquhan Estate. What started as two miners' cottages dating from 1745 has become an extended farmhouse with a well-proportioned elegance. Pale walls display contemporary artwork (some of it Elise's) and the sitting room is yours to share – deep red sofas, pale striped walls, shutters to keep out the wind, lamps to draw you in. Pretty bedrooms have long views and a period feel; one is furnished charmingly with a much-loved heirloom, an Edwardian suite; another has a sumptuous four-poster. In 2008 they started an apiary, in part a response to global concerns over 'colony collapse'... so far, the hive is thriving.

Price	£79. Singles from £49.50.
Rooms	2: 1 twin, 1 four-poster.
Meals	Packed lunch £5.50. Supper £15. Dinner £24.50. BYO.
Closed	November, January & February.
Directions	Langside Farm is 0.7 miles from the Dalry end of the B784. The B784 links the B780 Dalry-Kilbirnie road to the A760 Kilbirnie-Largs road.

Ethical Collection: Environment; Community; Food. See page 211.

Price band: C

Nick & Elise Quick
Langside Farm,
Dalry,
Ayrshire KA24 5JZ
Tel   +44 (0)1294 834402
Email   mail@langsidefarm.co.uk
Web   www.langsidefarm.co.uk

Anna's House

A peaceful house of contrast and artistry, through which flows a green creative energy. The field that spreads before the old farmhouse is the geothermal source of its heating, using electricity only for the pump; solar panels heat the water. Anna's love is the gardens: pine wood with hammock, secret lily pond, organic veg patch with gazebo, voluptuous borders, wildlife in thick hedges. Ken the music-lover has designed a soaring 'concert hall' extension: a 30-foot-high living space with a musician's gallery and acoustics for oratorios... and a wall of glass to tip you into the serenity of unlandscaped natural beauty and the lake. Gently cosmopolitan, hugely kind, Anna loves cooking and baking: one guest told of "breakfasts like wedding feasts". Bedrooms – each suite has its own sitting room and balcony with lovely views – are simply elegant with natural fabrics and organic paints, beautiful linen, mahogany doors, good showers; rural seclusion, the freshest food, the loveliest people – and a Toyota Prius to escort you to restaurants! *Local bike shop delivers bikes on request.*

Price	£80–£95. Singles £60.
Rooms	4: 1 double, 1 twin, 2 suites.
Meals	Pub-restaurant 0.5 miles (free taxi service).
Closed	Christmas & New Year.
Directions	From Belfast A20; A22 for Downpatrick; 3 miles after Comber, pass petrol station & pub on right; right onto Lisbarnett Rd 0.5 miles; right into private lane to end.

Ken & Anna Johnson
Anna's House,
Tullynagee, 35 Lisbarnett Road,
Comber, Co. Down BT23 6AW
Tel   +44 (0)2897 541566
Email   anna@annashouse.com
Web   www.annashouse.com

Ethical Collection: Environment; Food.
See page 211.

Price band: C

The Hermitage Cottage

Deeply different – and special. Sally has created a genuinely soulful environment on her wildlife refuge of 20 organic acres: a walking labyrinth; a deeply-bedded yurt for meditation courses, powered by solar panels; seated buddhas; secluded corners. With a deep-seated innocence and a love of her own Native American culture, Sally came to Tibetan Buddhism and is involved with the local inter-faith forum working to heal some of Northern Ireland's wounds. In this atmosphere, her weeny 'cottage' – a glorified lean-to attached to her family house – is aptly named: decked in Tibetan prayer flags, defended by a brass dragon door knocker, it is perfect for one frugal person in search of a week's birdsung serenity. Inside, you find basic living spaces: a single/double cell-like bedroom with high roughly hewn white walls, flagstones and a small desk, a windowless shower room, a neat little kitchen. The approach past someone else's scrap yard is anything but appealing, the furnishing is monastically spartan, the space minimal – but the people and the paradise garden are exceptional. *Hire the yurt for an event.*

Price	£240 per week.
Rooms	Cottage for 1-2.
Meals	Restaurant 1 mile.
Closed	Rarely.
Directions	From Saintfield for Ballynahinch. After speed limit ends, left into Drumnaconnell Road; at scrapyard, left up lane behind; 1st house on right. (Owners will collect from stations or airport.)

Ethical Collection: Environment.
See page 211.

Price band: B

Sally Taylor
The Hermitage Cottage,
14 Drumnaconnell Road,
Saintfield, Co. Down BT24 7NB

Tel	+44 (0)2897 510232
Email	sally.taylor803@btopenworld.com
Web	www.thehermitagecottage.com

Ardtarmon House

In the middle of nowhere, within 70 acres — and the views are magnetic. On a clear day the eye travels 60 miles out to sea; crashing surf is a short walk. The Henry family's home since an ancestor bought it in 1852, it grew to country house stature a century ago, the 'cloud-shrouded' top being familiarly known as the cosmos. Floors are painted, rugs faded, family oils hang on muted walls, breakfast tables are laid with Denby crockery. Stairs wind up to big spotless bedrooms with views — of tangled orchards and a giant cedar with a treehouse. Gentle, charming Charles and Christa are well on their way to environmental harmony. Their oil-thirsty heating has been impressively replaced with a biomass boiler, fed by a new fast-growing willow plantation: most of the house and half of the water is now heated by this renewable source and, with ten protected acres of biodiversity, free-range chickens, pigs, cattle and hearty seasonal, mostly organic meals they must have one of the most eco-sustainable places to stay in Ireland. The cottages are small and very simply furnished but warmed to perfection by a new woodchip boiler.

Price	€90-€120. Singles €65-€80. Cottages €200-€600 per week.
Rooms	4 + 5: 3 doubles, 1 family. 5 cottages for 2-6.
Meals	Dinner €30. Wine €15. Restaurant 8km.
Closed	Christmas & New Year.
Directions	Sligo N15 for Donegal, 8km to Drumcliffe; left for Carney, 1.5km. In village, signs to Raghley 7km; left at Dunleavy's shop 2.5km; gate lodge & drive on left.

Charles & Christa Henry
Ardtarmon House,
Ballinfull, Co. Sligo
Tel   +353 (0)71 9163156
Email   enquiries@ardtarmon.com
Web   www.ardtarmon.com

Ethical Collection: Environment; Food.
See page 211.

Price band: D

Ballin Temple

Tom and Pam took a radical turn from life in the city to develop the family estate – a veritable nature sanctuary. Sustainable thinkers, they have opened up the ancient woods, unearthed the buried garden aqueduct, built the first reed bed in the county and had the garden certified organic since 2000. They produce masses of delicious vegetables from artichokes to rhubarb, have reintroduced old potato varieties and let the chickens and ducks roam freely. They also practice and teach yoga, design and deliver holistic retreats and offer lifestyle transformation courses – why not book into one before you go? Guests stay in comfortable cottages that evoke memories of an Ireland of long ago, and the views across the valley are stunning. The estate wood is harvested to fuel the wood-burners of these open-hearted hideaway homes (there's 'space heating' too!), and the water comes from artesian wells. Stroll, or fish, along the banks of the river, mountain bike along narrow paths, be enveloped by peace in 70 acres of magical woods, and plant a tree before you go. A living, loving temple to life.

Price	From €26 p.p. (€500 per week for 2).
Rooms	2 cottages for 3-4.
Meals	Restaurant 3km.
Closed	Never.
Directions	From Carlow, N81 to Tullow, then to Ardattin & follow signs. Map & detailed directions on booking.

Ethical Collection: Environment; Community; Food.
See page 211.

Price band: B

The Butler Family
Ballin Temple,
Ardattin, Co. Carlow
Tel   +353 (0)59 9155037
Email   manager@ballintemple.com
Web   www.ballintemple.com

Kinvara Suites

One of the most picturesque villages in Ireland – and we have Elizabeth to thank for much of its preservation. She began with recording Kinvara's heritage in the form of guided walks; now, with the help of the council, she has restored (and transformed) the quiet harbour. Visit the old grain store on the waterfront, now a wonderful coffee shop and gallery celebrating local art and crafts. Close by, in a once-derelict hayloft, are two beautifully designed 'suites', under which are studios for Elizabeth's organic bodywrap treatments made from locally harvested seaweed. The top suite has a higher ceiling but both are stunning and clever: everything you need here in one large light room with high, quirky windows and pale wooden floors. A hub in the middle separates living area from sleeping and contains on one side a modern shower room and on the other a dazzling kitchen. Not your stereotypical green place but a worthy candidate nonetheless owing to Elizabeth's work in the locality and your chance to experience it first hand. Next on her list is a walkway along the wildflower bay.

Price	€500-€700 per week (3 nights €390).
Rooms	2 suites for 2.
Meals	Restaurants nearby.
Closed	Rarely.
Directions	From Shannon, N18 north. From Galway, N18 south to Kilcolgan; then N67 to Kinvara. Kinvara Suites are visible from main street on left-hand side.

Elizabeth Murphy
Kinvara Suites,
The Courtyard, Lower Main Street,
Kinvara, Co. Galway

Tel	+353 (0)91 637760
Email	murphystore@kinvara.com
Web	www.kinvarasuites.com

Ethical Collection: Community.
See page 211.

Price band: C

The Phoenix

Bohemian meets gypsy meets Arabian nights and they all decided to dance because… why wouldn't you? Somewhere in this exotic whirl is a two-foot high statue of St Theresa. Some years ago Lorna and Billy bought the house – a celebration of colour, wood, exposed stonework and rare plants – and have opened it up to open-minded devotees of organic vegetarian cooking: fresh breakfasts, tantalising lunches and seriously good dinners are served in a restaurant with colourful art on the walls. Lorna also sells wholefoods, gluten-free house products and organic wines and, in winter, runs cookery classes, organises salsa and Egyptian belly dancing classes, and encourages live music. There's also a room for workshops and therapeutic groups; the place fizzes with colour, life and energy. Bedrooms are large and comfortable, with spangled bedcovers and spotless bathrooms. As for the garden, it's gorgeous: wild areas for children to roam, treehouses, gypsy caravans (you can stay in them), a reed bed system and a productive vegetable patch. You're bang on the Inch beach road, so surfers will be happy.

Price	€80. Family room €80–€120. Single €45. Gypsy caravans €40. Chalet €450 per week.
Rooms	3 + 1: 1 double, 1 family, 1 single. Gypsy caravans for 2 + 2. Chalet for 2–3.
Meals	Lunch €5–€14. Dinner €18–€22.50. Packed lunch €8.
Closed	January.
Directions	From Castlemaine, R561 west for Dingle & Boolteens for 6km. House on right by road.

Ethical Collection: Environment; Community; Food.
See page 211.

Price band: C

Lorna & Billy Tyther
The Phoenix,
Shanahill East,
Castlemaine, Co. Kerry

Tel	+353 (0)66 9766284
Email	phoenixtyther@hotmail.com
Web	www.thephoenixorganic.com

Ballyroon Mountain

Spectacularly remote, in one of the last inhabited spots before Europe sinks into the Atlantic, Ballyroon ('secret place' in Irish) lives in the drama of plunging ocean and mountainous peninsulas. Friendly, sophisticated Roger and Sue – ex-cameraman and garden designer – came to this rugged hillside to farm and breathe clearer air. The little stone bothy beyond the main house is your cosy mountain cabin: one large bed-sitting room, simply, thoughtfully furnished with stone, timber and a thick woolly rug, the bed raised to catch the view, and your own garden. As natural as the best, Ballyroon is organic in all but certificate (paperwork too heavy, fee too high). Pigs provide rashers and delicious sausages, Angus cattle give the beef, bees harvest the hillsides for your honey. Hard work produces fresh chemical-free veg and fruit, the conservatory gathers heat, renewable woods grow the fuel, delightful donkeys carry it. Take all day to explore their 36 varied acres, walk the Sheep's Head and Poet's Ways, feel how every minute counts. You will come to love this retreat from urban frazzle as much as they do.

Price	€80-€100.
Rooms	1 double.
Meals	Dinner €30. BYO wine. 24hrs notice required. Restaurant 9km.
Closed	Rarely.
Directions	Directions on booking.

Roger & Sue Goss
Ballyroon Mountain,
Kilcrohane, Bantry, Co. Cork

Tel	+353 (0)27 67940
Email	info@ballyroonmountain.com
Web	www.ballyroonmountain.com

Ethical Collection: Environment; Food.
See page 211.

Price band: C

Hagal Healing Farm

Be greeted by homemade scones – and Fred, a spring of lavender behind one ear, a twinkle in his eye. Hagal is different, marvellously different. It always was: the farmhouse was built 150 years ago by one man in 40 days. At its heart is a tree trunk around which chunky polished oak steps spiral, with similarly polished branches acting as grab rails on the walls. Rooms flow from conservatory to kitchen to large low living area warmed by hemp plaster: simple, neat. Take lemon balm tea under the huge old vine in the conservatory among candles, jingling buddha chimes and lots of harmony, retreat into a secluded corner of the beautiful garden, left natural like everything here; insects hum, birds trill. Seating is low, ethnic and tempting; the chill-out room with white sofas has breathtaking views of Bantry Bay. Hagal is New Age heaven, run by gentle Dutch folk – Fred the garden-lover, Janny the yoga teacher, both deeply involved in the boundless natural energy of this land. Sun heats water; reed beds look after waste. Eat subtly spiced organic vegetarian food, or learn to cook it yourself. *Ask about weekend courses.*

Price	€70. Singles €50-€60. Full-board from €75 p.p.
Rooms	4 doubles.
Meals	Lunch €17. Dinner, 3 courses, €28. BYO wine. Book ahead.
Closed	Rarely.
Directions	From Bantry for Glengariff; right after Esso petrol station at Donemark; 12km of winding road; left at Hagal Farm sign.

Ethical Collection: Environment; Food.
See page 211.

Price band: C

Janny & Fred Wieler
Hagal Healing Farm,
Coomleigh, Bantry, Co. Cork
Tel   +353 (0)27 66179
Email   hagalhealingfarm@eircom.net
Web   www.hagalholistichealth.com

Gort-Na-Nain Vegetarian Guest House & Organic Farm

Just ask a ruddy-cheeked old boy the way to Gort-Na-Nain – you're most likely within touching distance of its hill-proud seat. Mists rise to uncover the new house, a distant sea and a lovingly cultivated market garden of organic riches that supplies some of the best restaurants in Cork. Ultan and Lucy's ecological vision doesn't stop at mouthwatering vegetarian food (try the parsnip tortellini) but reaches to planting hedgerows and protecting indigenous woodland. The sun supplies hot water and wood-burners heat the house, stocky fireplaces spreading from its country kitchen heart – a gorgeous smelling hub where something is always bubbling above dark flagstones. Across the hallway is the shared sitting room, fresh decorated with light oak floors, comfy sofas, wooden chests and Lucy's handmade curtains; another pair, golden with rich red flowers, frames a bedroom window. There is uncluttered comfort throughout, either on king-size sleigh beds or on a clever zip-link double/twin covered in deepening shades of lavender. Peace comes dropping slow, to borrow Yeats; here it stays the night.

Price	€85–€95. Singles €60.
Rooms	3: 2 doubles, 1 twin/double.
Meals	Dinner, 3 courses & glass of wine, €30. Packed lunch €10. Pub & restaurant 1.5km.
Closed	Rarely.
Directions	From Cork on Kinsale road, R600. Left between two pubs at Belgooly; signs to Oysterhaven; at x-roads, turn towards Nohoval; 1st left, 3rd house on right.

Lucy Stewart & Ultan Walsh
Gort-Na-Nain Vegetarian Guest House & Organic Farm, Ballyherkin, Nohoval, Kinsale, Co. Cork

Tel	+353 (0)21 4770647
Email	lucy@gortnanain.com
Web	www.gortnanain.com

Ethical Collection: Environment; Food. See page 211.

Price band: C

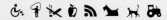

Entry 52 Map 1

Woodbrook House

The long sweeping drive, the Georgian house protected by massive old hardwoods, tucked under the snowcapped mountain, the pillared entrance flanked by two marble lions... so far, so Anglo-Irish. The hall, lit by two-storey windows and with a Mediterranean-toned frieze, suggests a warmer clime. Giles and Alexandra are no strangers to the wider world; she is half-Italian, he capped a diplomatic career as British ambassador to Venezuela. They toured Italy and India before starting an eco restoration on their intriguing, 1770s, somewhat ramshackle house with Ireland's only 'flying staircase' which quivers as you climb. Lions from Rome and painted furniture from Rajasthan came home with them; bedrooms are big, family-friendly, unposh; some have balconies for long parkland views. Giles, well-travelled and well-read, has strong convictions, a wry humour and is a leading Irish Green. Roof-nested tubes capture sunshine to heat showers; the wood-pellet boiler burns for toasty times indoors and Woodbrook was host in 2007 and 2008 to the wildly sustainable Irish Green Gathering.

Price	€150–€170. Singles €95–€105.
Rooms	4: 2 doubles, 1 twin; 1 family with separate bathroom.
Meals	Dinner €50. Wine from €15.
Closed	November–April. Groups off season by arrangement.
Directions	Enniscorthy R702 to Kiltealy. Through village towards Rathnure, 2.5km; left down small lane with tall trees; entrance, not signed, 300m, on left down drive.

Ethical Collection: Environment; Food.
See page 211.

Price band: E

Giles & Alexandra FitzHerbert
Woodbrook House,
Killanne, Enniscorthy,
Co. Wexford

Tel +353 (0)53 9255114
Email fitzherbert@eircom.net
Web www.woodbrookhouse.ie

Western Europe

Wilgenhof

The prettily named 'Willow Farm' is surrounded by poplars and willows and a profusion of vegetation including some large greenhouses – two of which make bright dining rooms amid the tomatoes. Wilgenhof is in the driest region of Belgium and when the sun shines this is smallholding heaven, with paths winding their way through the sprawly jungle and animals to meet on the way: ponies, sheep, goats, rabbits, hens, a pig. Ponds are safely fenced, everything is organic, there's a reed bed, piles of firewood and heaps of solar panels. Inside one of several buildings are guest bedrooms with plain dark furniture and new pine, and fly-screens across windows, while corridors are hung with carpets and old paintings; the owners, keen travellers, once sold Asian crafts. Now they are long-standing members of VELT, Belgium's ecology council; paints are non-toxic, showers are low-flow, imported food is fairtrade. They are also Slow Food members so communal mealtimes are leisurely and long and almost all the meat and veg are home-reared and home-grown – delicious. Set off on the bikes, or visit Bruges and Ghent for the day.

Price	€60–€82. Apartment €300–€460 p.w. House €600–€950 p.w.
Rooms	6 + 2: 2 doubles, 1 twin, 3 suites for 5. Apartment for 5. House for 10.
Meals	Dinner €15. Wine from €9.
Closed	Rarely.
Directions	E40 Ostend-Brussels, exit Aalter; N44 to Maldegem, exit Kleit (village south of Maldegem); signed (3km).

Ethical Collection: Environment; Food.
See page 211.

Price band: C

Rita Hendrickx
Wilgenhof,
Pot & Zuidhoutstraat 4,
9990 Maldegem

Tel	+32 (0)50 71 53 66
Email	hendrickx.wilgenhof@skynet.be
Web	www.wilgenhof.be

Lomolen B&B

Breezy, blithe and self-assured is your hostess, crisp and peaceful are your rooms, and breakfasts are bountiful and organic. This may not be the most charismatic of addresses, next to a residential estate, but it all feels relaxing and rural and has been most thoughtfully done. At right angles to the modern family house is a new eco-friendly brick barn for guests: triple bedroom, shared sitting room and terrace on the ground floor, two family rooms up above. From the back, views extend over a young and neatly lawned orchard to neighbouring pastures where horses graze in meadows bordered by willows; weathered cobbles pave terraces and the odd agricultural artefact has been artfully placed. It is all perfectly safe for children – there's table footie in the old barn and a colourful hammock. As for 'greenery': loos are dual-flush, insulation is top notch, lighting is low energy, showers are solar-heated, plaster and paints are chemical-free and the laundry uses harvested rainwater. After a day discovering Bruges, Ghent or the coast, how reassuring to return to a welcoming family and beds cosy with thick duvets.

Price	€78-€105.
Rooms	3: 2 family rooms for 4-5, 1 triple.
Meals	Dinner, 3 courses, €20-€25. Wine from €12. Restaurant 1km.
Closed	Never.
Directions	Ostende A10 to E40 dir. Brussels-Aalter. N409 to Lotenhulle. At village, left to Nevelstraat, right to Kleine Lijkstraat; right to Lomolenstraat. Signed. Or, by train to Aalter via Bruges or Ghent.

	Francis & Kathleen Huysman-Barbier
	Lomolen B&B,
	Lomolenstraat 112,
	9880 Aalter
Tel	+32 (0)9 371 95 15
Email	stay@lomolenlogies.be
Web	www.lomolenlogies.be

Ethical Collection: Environment. See page 211.

Price band: C

Hof Van Steelant

In a sympathetically renovated, edge-of-village farmhouse – four miles from the centre of resplendent Bruges – live Lucia and Fons: the loveliest people. She is a nurse and Green Party member, he is an artist and organic vegetable-grower (output: 100 tons a year) whose ethically run farm employs society's marginalised; miraculously they find time to nurture four flaxen-haired children and their B&B guests. On the ground floor of this noble old house are two pleasingly simple bedrooms: a plain pine bed, a country antique, a sheep fleece on a rosy terracotta floor, an abstract painting on a white wall. The loos are rainwater-flushed, the living area has beams painted a sober blue, and rush-seated chairs at a long table. Outside are a playhouse and big round sandpit all children may share, alongside Fons's bright sculptures and vegetable patch brimming with produce. In the meadow are sheep, donkeys and hens – source of eggs for breakfast feasts: homemade tomato and basil bread, fabulous jams, organic fruits and cheeses, fairtrade coffees and teas. Simple living at its richest.

Ethical Collection: Community; Food.
See page 211.

Price band: C

Price	€50–€60.
Rooms	2: 1 family room for 2-3, 1 twin sharing bathroom. Cots & inflatable beds available.
Meals	Restaurant 100m.
Closed	Never.
Directions	From Bruges A10 exit 7B Loppem. Right at church to Rijselstraat; 50m. House on left with red iron gate. Or, train to Bruges & bus 72 or 74 to Loppem.

Family Dewitte Breekelmans
Hof Van Steelant,
Rijselsestraat 17, Zedelgem,
8210 Loppem

Tel	+32 (0)50 59 96 80
Email	reservation@hofvansteelant.be
Web	www.hofvansteelant.be

Entry 56 Map 3

Jessenhofke: Beer, Bed & Breakfast

Here is a friendly B&B with an ultra-modern appeal. The house is semi-detached and architect-designed, so you get solar panels and condensation boilers, harvested rainwater and low-flush loos. Walls are painted in eco-friendly neutrals and your young hosts look after you beautifully: Gert, who works in IT and has an organic microbrewery close by, and Christel, trained in massage and aromatherapy. All feels fresh and inviting and the guest rooms – 'Hop' and 'Barley' – are immaculate, spacious and serene. Floors are carpeted, pillows are bamboo fibre, duvets are rose petal-strewn. Note the double has its Starck-designed bath in the bedroom itself; the family room has an en suite shower. Towelling robes are neatly folded, bubbles are herbal; there's a laid-back but luxurious feel. On the landing are microwave and fridge, in the small garden, apples to pick, a sandpit, treehouse and big blow-up pool. Bike into Hasselt – a big bustling town, largely car-free – or, if you time it right, be a brewer for a day. In any case, Gert will treat you to tastings. Breakfasts, too, are as organic as can be. *Minimum stay two nights.*

Price	€90. Discounts for children.
Rooms	2: 1 double, 1 family room. Extra beds available.
Meals	Occasional dinner with beer, €20. Restaurants 3km.
Closed	January–April.
Directions	Directions on booking.

Gert & Christel Jordens-Putzeys
Jessenhofke: Beer, Bed & Breakfast,
Jessenhofstraat 8,
3511 Kuringen-Hasselt

Tel   +32 (0)11 25 56 99
Email   bed@jessenhofke.be
Web   www.jessenhofke.be

Ethical Collection: Environment; Food.
See page 211.

Price band: C

Entry 57   Map 3

Energite

Here are three pristine-perfect, newly converted, ecologically sound gîtes in a big old L-shaped farm building in the Belgian Ardennes. And the Ardennes are lovely, with their undulating woody hills, pockets of copse and grazing meadows... wake to chirruping birds and tractor hum. The owner lives in Namur but has a meeter-and-greeter who shows you the ropes: where to shop, how to hire bicycles, caterers, babysitters... and offers tailormade tours at a price. The three gîtes can be let separately or as one; the most private, with its own entrance, is single storey with doors wide enough to accommodate a wheelchair. The others are adjacent, and identical, their living spaces down and their bedrooms up. Furniture is functional, nothing is superfluous, floors are tiled, colours are bright, kitchens are super-equipped and linen and towels can be supplied. All is super-insulated, heating is low-energy, paints are pure, there's wetlands for sewage and solar panels are in the offing. Shared are the common room with table football and home cinema, and the run-around garden with barbecue, swings and stream.

Price	€413 per week.
Rooms	3 apartments for 6.
Meals	Restaurant 5km.
Closed	Never.
Directions	N4 exit Barnière Hinck & Bertogne to N826 dir. St Ode; left to Tillet, past church on right. Right at x-roads dir. Acul. Right to Chisogne. Entrance on right at bottom of hill. Or, by train Brussels-Luxembourg to Libramont; taxi/bus arranged by owner.

Ethical Collection: Environment.
See page 211.

Price band: B

	Nathaly Laitat-Pereaux
	Energite, Chisogne 5,
	6680 Sainte-Ode
Tel	+32 (0)81 22 16 64
Email	energite@sudepervier.be
Web	www.energite.be

Les Hauts

From a hillside perch above the village, peer across the bay to the mystical outline of Mont St Michel; then walk there (or ride on horseback) along the coastal path. The bedrooms at Les Hauts are airy and light – try the 'Eisenhower' (yes, he slept here) or the balconied 'Tulipes' with its super Art Deco furniture; the original tap-making owner left some magnificent basins and fittings. The Leroys have a passion for the environment and are successfully finding ways of greening their 1830s chateau. The roof has full insulation, all-natural materials have been used in the restoration, they've added solar thermals for hot water, dug deep to retrieve the geothermal warmth for heating, and sunk a rainwater harvesting tank under the tennis courts. They farm organically, too (although the farm is some miles away). They are also happy for you to buy their produce and use their kitchen. Concerts are held in the lovely stepped garden, visits to Mont St Michel are arranged. And your hosts' active participation in local conservation makes for interesting chat over breakfast, a help-yourself buffet feast.

Price	€95-€110. Singles €85. Suites €140-€240.
Rooms	5: 1 double, 1 twin, 3 suites for 2-4.
Meals	Dinner €18-€38. Wine €10-€25. Book ahead. Restaurants 5-min walk.
Closed	Rarely.
Directions	From Cherbourg, N13 to Valognes; D2 to Coutances; D971 to Granville; D911 (along coast) to Jullouville; on to Carolles & St Jean Le Thomas (6.5km from Jullouville). Property entrance at end of village on right.

André & Suzanne Leroy
Les Hauts,
7 avenue de la Libération,
50530 St Jean Le Thomas

Tel	+33 (0)2 33 60 10 02
Email	contact@chateau-les-hauts.com
Web	www.chateau-les-hauts.com

Ethical Collection: Environment; Food.
See page 211.

Price band: C

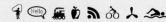

La Métairie

The gorgeous country garden is the real glory of this 300-year-old farmhouse. To one side of the drive are beds spilling over with organically grown vegetables, clustered flowers and a grapevine; to the other, fruit trees and lawned spaces. A chestnut and thatch summerhouse is the backdrop for memorable evening meals – largely organic, carefully flavoured and garnished with home-grown herbs; the gluten-free bread is delicious. Hosts Jon and Liz, who settled in France eight years ago from Derbyshire, are delightful, unpretentious and fun. They have planted dill for the swallowtail butterflies, lemon verbena for tea and 50 new trees; and there are red squirrels. Inside, a sunny yellow kitchen-diner that's cosy and convivial, and cheerful bedrooms whose windows open on to the couple's herd of sheep on the hills. A wood-burning stove in a granite fireplace warms the family suite, while the barn roof fills a huge rainwater collection tank (a wind turbine is on its way); the apartment for two forms part of a two-storey barn. It's a swift 20 minutes to beaches and Mont St Michel – you could even cycle there.

Price	€60. Suite €80.
	Apartment €290–€360 per week.
Rooms	3 + 1: 1 double with separate bath;
	1 family suite (1 double, 1 twin).
	Apartment for 2.
Meals	Dinner with wine, €23.
	Restaurant 6km.
Closed	Christmas & New Year.
Directions	D47 from Avranches dir. Isigny Le Buat.
	Intersection with D106 after 10km;
	left to La Boulouze & immed. right
	fork. After 300m, house sign on left.

Ethical Collection: Environment; Food.
See page 211.

Price band: C

Jon & Liz Bushell
La Métairie,
50220 Marcilly

Tel	+33 (0)2 33 58 20 14
Email	bushell@west-telecom.com
Web	www.lametairie.co.uk

Earthship Perrine

Inspired by the off-grid 'earthships' of American eco-visionary Michael Reynolds, the Trotts have created their very own. Set against a great mound of earth in a field on the edge of a Normandy village, it looks more greenhouse than house. Fully sustainable, aesthetically pleasing, its chunky glazed façade facing south, the house has been constructed from an ingenious mix of earth-packed tyres and discarded cans, granite boulders and reclaimed oak. The radically green Earthship Perrine heats and cools itself naturally with solar thermal dynamics and harvests its own rain. Three cosy bedrooms feed off a corridor lush with plants; the shower room and homely kitchen/living areas lie at the far end. Walls are smooth tinted clay, glass bottles create vibrant spots of light, furniture is minimal, linen is snowy white, and a Godin burner glows on cold nights. Outside are a furnished patio and big round sandpit; a permaculture garden and wind turbine will follow. Gaze on cottages and fields, listen to birdsong and horses, bring bikes, boots and biodegradable shampoos – the water must stay pure for the plants!

Price	From £600 (sterling) per week.
Rooms	House for 6 (1 four-poster, 1 double, 1 twin).
Meals	Restaurant 500m.
Closed	Never.
Directions	A84 Caen-Rennes exit 42 Vire. D524 to Tinchebray; D22 & D23 to Ger. Right at 1st junction; left at 1st r'bout; right at 2nd; 300m on right. Or, by bus from Caen ferry to Vire & bus to Sourdeval; then 15-min taxi.

Kevan Trott
Earthship Perrine,
Perrine, Route de Barenton,
50850 Ger

Tel	+44 (0)1273 245055
Email	kevan@earthship.co.uk
Web	www.earthship-france.com

Ethical Collection: Environment;
Community. See page 211.

Price band: C

Perché dans le Perche

Toss the suitcases into the barrow, trundle through the mown grass and there she rises: an amazing treehouse on the edge of a meadow. The grand old chestnut tree does not support the hemp-insulated two-storey structure on stilts but sweetly embraces it – and a leafy branch grows through the corner of one room. Inside is spacious and gorgeous: floors warmed by colourful rugs, beds topped by cushions and pillows, double-glazed windows protected by meshes and blinds. Be enchanted by nesting birds, long views, glittering night skies. You get china, cutlery, microwave, toaster, fridge, maps, books, games, WiFi, electricity, shower, deckchairs for decks, summer kitchen, hammocks and swings. Soaps are organic and honey-based, cleaning products eco, and Claire delivers a basket of local breakfast goodies to your door. She and Ivan are creating a wildlife-rich wetland area fed by water from natural springs and have installed a reed bed filter system: "a project for people" with which local schoolchildren are involved. As for Le Perche, it is big, empty, hilly, and overflows with history.

Price	€150 for 2. Extra person €20. €700-€1,200 per week.
Rooms	Treehouse for 5 (1 double, bunks for 3, kitchenette & shower).
Meals	Restaurant 5km.
Closed	December-February.
Directions	From La Ferté Bernard, D2 dir. Mamers. After 10km, right to Bellou-le-Trichard; in village, right at x-roads, 2km, then left after water tower; at bottom of track.

Ethical Collection: Environment; Community; Food.
See page 211.

Price band: D

Claire Stickland
Perché dans le Perche,
La Renardière,
61130 Bellou le Trichard

Tel	+33 (0)2 33 25 57 96
Email	perchedansleperche@gmail.com
Web	www.perchedansleperche.com

La Maison du Vert

Debbie and Daniel's restaurant is vegetarian (or vegan), gourmet and much-admired; organic wine and cider wash down delicious worldly flavours. Vert is the house name and green is the splendid garden: two sloping terraced acres and a pleasing organic kitchen plot that supplies all the salads and half of the vegetables. At the lower end, where once a small public washing house stood, is a large natural pond fed by a spring and a haven for birds (cirl buntings have been sighted), a tranquil place where tables and chairs are set out under large shrub bushes where one can watch the wildlife. And there's a young orchard, flourishing under permaculture principles. Bedrooms, on the first floor and reached by a twisty staircase, have lovely views over the garden or the rolling wooded countryside. For junior visitors there is a large enclosure with pet rabbits and a flock of free-range organic hens kind enough to provide all the eggs needed. Debbie and Daniel are more like friends than hosts – expect a big welcome. *Garden events help fund the restoration of local historic buildings.*

Price	€59-€69.
Rooms	3: 2 doubles, 1 family room.
Meals	Dinner, 3 courses, €29.
	Wine from €11.85.
Closed	October-Easter.
Directions	D579 Lisieux-Vimoutiers; D979 for Alençon for 5km; left D12 for L'Aigle. In Ticheville, left opp. church, hotel 20m on right.

Debbie & Daniel Armitage
La Maison du Vert,
Le Bourg, 61120 Ticheville

Tel	+33 (0)2 33 36 95 84
Email	mail@maisonduvert.com
Web	www.maisonduvert.com

Ethical Collection: Community; Food.
See page 211.

Price band: C

Ty Bois

Leaving tiny hamlets behind, you're on the track leading down to the river; then a steep climb up, through a garden lined with agapanthus flowers. The wooden chalet at the summit, modestly fringed by forest trees, sits on a river plot in the Parc Régional d'Armorique and the views are breathtaking, from house and terrace. Installed by a charitable company that employs handicapped workers, sourced from local cypress trees, that terrace is stunning. Inside is just as good. Minimalist bedrooms are decorated with panache: neutral tones and deep purple blushes, piles of linen pillows on French brocante beds. The friendly ground floor embraces kitchen, dining area and salon in Alpine fashion, with furniture coming from a local social enterprise. Big bathrooms exude a luxurious simplicity; the compact kitchen, stocked with eco products, has stylish taupe cupboards and zinc surfaces. Claire and Andrew live nearby and have removed invasive laurel from sensitive woods; fires are fuelled from fallen logs. As for the Crozon peninsula, it's a joy to explore – make the most of the kayaks provided.

Price	£495-£1,250 (sterling) per week.
Rooms	House for 6 (2 doubles, 1 twin/double).
Meals	Restaurant 3km.
Closed	Never.
Directions	N165 exit Le Faou/Rosnoen, signed. In village, right to Belvedere & Pont de Terenez; 2km; left after house with blue shutters down steep lane to river. On left.

Ethical Collection: Environment.
See page 211.

Price band: C

Claire Bernard
Ty Bois,
Kergadalen, 29590 Rosnoen
Tel   +33 (0)2 98 55 29 26
Email   frenchberry@orange.fr
Web   www.frenchberry.com

La Besnardière

English Joyce, calm personified, brims with knowledge about aromatherapy and all things horticultural. She's been organic for 30 years and everything she grows is chemical-free. "The preparation of a guest's meal commences when I put the fork in the ground," says she; delicious all-vegetarian or vegan dishes come from produce that was in the ground half an hour before landing on your plate. Vegetables grow in abundance here and Joyce is an expert gardener. She welcomes art, yoga and meditation workshops to her meditation room, and shares this fresh, comforting and comfortable home with generosity. Beams spring everywhere in the 500-year-old farmhouse – mind your head! – and the two big, warm, book-filled bedrooms are tucked under the rafters, one with steps to a courtyard below. Be charmed by log fires, a sofa'd sitting room with jolly throws, a reading snug with silk cushions, a garden full of wild flowers, a donkey, goats, ducks, hens and views. No remarkable steps to green her house yet but her organic approach merits our recommendation and we'd be surprised if you weren't delighted.

Price	€60.
Rooms	2: 1 double, 1 triple, sharing bathroom.
Meals	Dinner (vegetarian or vegan) with wine, €20.
Closed	Rarely.
Directions	A11 to Durtal; D138 to Fougeré; D217 for Baugé; 1.5km, house on left.

Joyce Rimell
La Besnardière,
Route de Baugé, 49150 Fougeré
Tel   +33 (0)2 41 90 15 20
Email   rimell.joyce@wanadoo.fr
Web   www.holiday-loire.com

Ethical Collection: Food.
See page 211.

Price band: C

Entry 65   Map 2

La Chouannière – La Cabane

In a fairytale woodland setting, a little log cabin on stilts. Once an observation studio in Russia, later salvaged by Gilles and Patricia (it has lamb's wool insulation and hemp floors), it comes with a balcony that's perfect for spotting wildlife while supping al fresco: birds, boar, game and deer wander amongst the trees. Cute and comfortable, the cabin is perfumed with pinewood and furnished with a sitting area and kitchenette, a ship's bed behind curtains, a small power shower and an antique portmanteau trunk for your garb. There's table d'hôtes in the stables of your hosts' 16th-century house so book in for dinner, then take a stroll round the woodland gardens, complete with old pigeonnier and new bakery; here Gilles makes croissants, pastries, brioche and bread. Pâtés, rillettes, aperitifs and jams are homemade too, and there's a summer kitchen for you to share. Walking and biking tours start from the door: trails take you through the forests and past wildlife ponds into the Anjou. And the bubbles of the jacuzzi should entice you home. *Minimum stay two-four nights.*

Price	€75 (€525 per week).
Rooms	1 cabin for 2 (1 double, kitchenette & shower).
Meals	Picnic lunch/dinner, with wine, €10 p.p. Summer kitchen. Restaurant 7km.
Closed	January.
Directions	From Saumur N147 for Longué; right D938 for Baugé; in Jumelles, left at church for Brion; signed.

Ethical Collection: Environment.
See page 211.

Price band: C

Patricia & Gilles Patrice
La Chouannière – La Cabane,
Domaine des Hayes,
49250 Brion
Tel　　+33 (0)2 41 80 21 74
Email　chouanniere@loire-passion.com
Web　　www.loire-passion.com

Château de l'Enclos – Kota Cabana

Indefatigable Monsieur makes his own brandy, works with the community (schools adore the tree trail) and, with lively Madame, nurtures château and parkland almost single-handedly. Chancing upon a Finnish designer who introduced him to pinewood Lapland *kotas* he set about building his own, suspended between a Lebanon cedar and two sequoias. Ascend the circular, 40-step staircase to two lovely, cosy, resin-scented rooms and an octagonal deck with views over parkland and pets (llamas, sheep, donkey, hens). Unbroken countryside stretches beyond – glorious. The bed is canopied, the rug is seagrass, the colours are creamy, the washbasin and loo fit perfectly and the telescope zooms in on the wildlife. At the appointed hour, your hosts ring the brass bell below and attach a splendid breakfast basket to the pulley (and other meals, and champagne…). In the grounds, two wells help water the animals whose manure feeds the organic vegetables. Rain is harvested, condensation-based heating is energy-efficient and all is recycled that can be. Brûlon, "petite cité de charactère", is so close you can stroll there.

Price	€150.
Rooms	Tree cabin for 2. Shower close by.
Meals	Basket dinner with wine, €30. Restaurant 6km.
Closed	Never.
Directions	From A81 Le Mans-Laval; exit 1 to Brûlon. Château on right at end of town. Signed.

Annie-Claude & Jean-Claude Guillou
Château de l'Enclos – Kota Cabana,
72350 Brûlon

Tel	+33 (0)2 43 92 17 85
Email	jean-claude.guillou5@wanadoo.fr
Web	www.chateau-enclos.com

Ethical Collection: Environment; Food.
See page 211.

Price band: D

Les Chambres Vertes

Sophie's artistic eye and environmental awareness blend art and ecology as though they should always be together. From the bedroom decoration (original wattle and daub) to her lime-rendering, from the non-VOC oatmeal hues to the hemp insulation, Sophie has made a beautiful home in harmony with nature. Flowers fill the quadrangle formed by the 16th–19th-century house that Sophie has carefully restored; a fountain adds coolness. Your rooms are in the former stables opposite Sophie's house, each with a slate porch for shelter. Outside the quadrangle is a covered patio, overlooking countryside, for summer drinks and delicious all-organic meals; vegetables come freshly picked from Sophie's natural garden. All this is just a stone's throw from the village. The bedrooms, on the ground floor, are uncluttered and exquisitely simple, with attractive no-frills bathrooms. The sun heats the showers; wood chips service the underfloor heating; clean energy powers the lights; Sophie has achieved something very special in the Loire and it's for sharing. Natural, artistic, delightful.

Price	€59–€63.
Rooms	3: 2 doubles, 1 twin.
Meals	Dinner with wine, €24.
Closed	Occasionally.
Directions	A10 from Paris, exit Blois for Châteauroux D956, 15km; left just before village sign Cormeray; 800m, left. 1st house on left.

Ethical Collection: Environment; Food.
See page 211.

Price band: C

Sophie Gélinier
Les Chambres Vertes,
Le Clos de la Chartrie,
41120 Cormeray

Tel	+33 (0)2 54 20 24 95
Email	sophie@chambresvertes.net
Web	www.chambresvertes.net

Le Bouchot

Come not for luxury but for deep country authenticity – and to make friends with a generous, charming, free-thinking family who gave up Paris for this lush corner of France. Here they spread their organic philosophy, literally: they banned chemicals on arrival and use homemade nettle fertiliser instead. Gradually nature on the farm is "reclaiming its place". Their reforestation campaign has been recognised by the UN – hundreds of trees have been planted and micro-fauna is encouraged. Anne and Jean-Philippe, a writer and lecturer on conservation, have also restored and eco-converted the run-down 300-year-old farm, insulating it with hemp, wattle and daub and adding wood-burning stoves, organic breakfasts and friendly pets. Bedrooms in outbuildings round a central courtyard are wood-clad with sloping ceilings, rudimentary furnishings, mix and match bed linen and the odd rug. Dinner is in the kitchen-diner – or in the barns, when there are campers. Learn how to run an organic kitchen garden; meet the horses, hens, donkeys, peacocks and sheep; admire some of the best conservation in Europe.

Price	€55–€65.
Rooms	3: 1 family room for 3, 1 family room for 4, 1 suite for 2-7.
Meals	Dinner with wine, €25. Restaurant 2km.
Closed	Rarely.
Directions	Orléans A71 for Vierzon, exit 3 to Lamotte Beuvron; D23 & D55 to Pierrefitte sur Sauldre; right in church square onto D126 for Chaon; 1km to house.

Anne & Jean-Philippe Beau-Douëzy
Le Bouchot,
Route de Chaon,
41300 Pierrefitte sur Sauldre

Tel	+33 (0)2 54 88 01 00
Email	contact@lebouchot.net
Web	www.lebouchot.net

Ethical Collection: Environment.
See page 211.

Price band: C

Hôtel Les Orangeries

Even before you step inside, the long cool pool beneath the trees will convince you that these people have the finest sense of how to treat an old house and its surroundings. The harmony of the deep wooden deck, raw stone walls, giant baskets and orange trees draws you in; candles add magic by night. The young owners (he an architect) fell in love with the place and applied all their talent to giving it an 18th-century elegance in contemporary mood. Stripped oak doors, exposed stone walls, cool stone floors glow with loving care. Olivia has given each bedroom its own sense of uncluttered harmony; the quietest face the garden, the rest face the road and the split-level apartments are a delight. Water from the heavens to your shower is heated by the sun; linen is eco-certified; soft towels are woven from bamboo. Old-fashioned games have been resuscitated: croquet and skittles under the trees, billiards, backgammon, mahjong. Olivia speaks wonderful English and her enthusiasm for house, garden, animals (and you!) is catching. The hot chocolate – organic, of course – is the best you will ever have tasted.

Price	€65–€140. Apartments €105–€175.
Rooms	15: 11 doubles, 4 apartments for 4–5 (without kitchen).
Meals	Breakfast from €12.50. Dinner from €30. Wine from €18.
Closed	Rarely.
Directions	Exit Poitiers for Limoges on N147 to Lussac les Châteaux; 35km. Ask for route via Châtellerault if arriving from north.

Ethical Collection: Environment; Food.
See page 211.

Price band: C

Olivia & Jean-Philippe Gautier
Hôtel Les Orangeries,
12 avenue du Docteur Dupont,
86320 Lussac les Châteaux

Tel	+33 (0)5 49 84 07 07
Email	orangeries@wanadoo.fr
Web	www.lesorangeries.fr

Le Clos des Jardins – Le Four du Boulanger & Les Écuries

With its sunflower fields, honeystone walls and carthorses, the tiny village of Mandegault is a reminder of how rural France used to be. Life slows to a tranquil trot, a pace which English owners Alison and Francis have been more than happy to adopt at their 18th-century organic farmstead with its two little cottages. Hens and ducks potter in the courtyard (children may collect the eggs at feeding time), a family of rare black sheep grazes their garden. The couple have been equally respectful of local styles. In the two-floored 'Baker's Oven' – an old bakery – the original vaulted stone bread oven and authentic diamond-shaped *œil de bœuf* windows have been kept, while beautiful natural fabrics, oak beams and creamy stone walls create a mood of soothing elegance. Equal charm is present in the rustic, ground-floor 'Stables'. There's a shared games area with a small raised solar-heated pool and a delightful garden for Les Écuries (to share if the cottages are rented together); pick herbs and sprinkle them over the fresh organic vegetables the Hudsons supply. Great for families, and good value.

Price	Le Four £150–£495. Les Écuries £130–£455. Prices (sterling) per week.
Rooms	Le Four & Les Écuries sleep 4–6 each.
Meals	Dinner, 4 courses with wine, €18; by arrangement. Children under 10 eat free. Restaurant 3km.
Closed	Rarely. Long lets November–April only.
Directions	From D948 dir. Limoges, D737 signed Chef Boutonne, D1 then D109 signed Melleran. Left to Mandegault, 250m on right.

Francis & Alison Hudson
Le Clos des Jardins
Rue de la Cour, Mandegault,
79190 Melleran

Tel	+33 (0)5 49 29 65 31
Email	mandegault@aol.com
Web	www.ruralretreats.org

Ethical Collection: Environment; Food.
See page 211.

Price band: C

Entry 71   Map 2

Le Moulin de la Borderie

Come for a stylish renovated mill with a resident owl, a beautiful outdoor pool and modestly intellectual hosts (an ex-teacher and a doctor) who love their island and have made the first steps towards living sustainably upon it. A ground-source heat pump looks after the heating, island sunshine is collected in solar thermals for hot water, cleaning, painting and garden chemicals are banned, and Vanina's passion is to protect the island's forests and beaches. Behind smoke-blue shutters, floaty muslins frame tall windows among pastel hues of sand and aqua green. Hollyhocks romp in the lovely garden, and at breakfast a suspended sail keeps the sun off while you delight in galette charentaise, freshly picked garden tomatoes, bourrache, consoude and sweet-scented strawberries, island-grown. Discover the local seaweed bread, delicious with 'fleur de sel' butter. Dinner is probably catch of the day – squid, seabass or cooked oysters – then crème caramel and a magnificent view of the stars. Rent a bike locally; the island, once home to 120 windmills, is all yours.

Price	€70–€96.
Rooms	4: 2 doubles, each with separate bathroom; 1 double, 1 suite (1 double, 1 twin).
Meals	Dinner with wine, €25.
Closed	Rarely.
Directions	From Saintes, A10 for Île d'Oléron; after bridge for St Pierre d'O, 800m; at r'bout entering town, right Rue Pierre Loti; 5th turning on left, downhill, Rue de la République for 1km; mill on right.

Ethical Collection: Environment; Food.
See page 211.

Price band: C

Vanina Thiou
Le Moulin de la Borderie,
184 rue de la République,
17310 Saint Pierre d'Oléron

Mobile	+33 (0)6 80 45 60 42
Email	lemoulindevany@aol.com
Web	www.lemoulindelaborderie.com

La Geyrie – Gîte Maison

Gîte Maison is attached to the Dunns' house and shares their solar panels. This is a working farm: sheepdogs roam, cats doze, there are hens in the yard and a clutch of Jack Russells. Sheltered amongst the woods, even the goats have an eco-friendly home with solar panels and a reed bed system. Farmstead and countryside have a marvellously ancient feel, Peter and Louise are busy and committed and everyone may happily muck in. Dry-stone-walling students practise on the many tumbledown walls, young farmers learn how to milk the organic goats. Inside your cool gîte are classic limewash walls and terracotta floors, chairs are straight-backed, the sofa is small and a 1930s dresser houses the crockery – plain but genuine. Bedrooms and bathroom upstairs feed into each other with a fine-sized bedroom at the front dominated by an old fireplace and another at the back big enough for a double bed, two singles and bunks. Mattresses are new, cotton sheets are coloured, the bathroom is for everyone and the small kitchen even has a dishwasher! This is an outdoorsy place where free-range families will be happy.

Price	£260–£415 per week (sterling).
Rooms	Gîte for 4–8 (1 double, 1 quadruple + bunks).
Meals	Restaurant 9km.
Closed	Never.
Directions	Leave Angoulême direction Périgueux. At Mareuil follow signs to La Tour Blanche taking D99 for 9km. After La Chapelle Montabourlet, La Geyrie is 3rd hamlet on left. House on left.

Louise & Peter Dunn
La Geyrie – Gîte Maison,
Cercles, 24320 Verteillac

Tel	+33 (0)5 53 91 15 15
Email	peter.dunn@wanadoo.fr
Web	www.lageyrie.com

Ethical Collection: Environment.
See page 211.

Price band: B

Château Haut Garrigue

The Feelys pursued the dream: to buy a vineyard in France. They chanced upon the commune of Saussignac, noted for its organic producers and its dessert wines. Three years down the line they produce a gorgeous white sauvignon "with a wild, earthy streak on the nose" and an equally praised merlot and rosé; in 2009 they win organic certification from EcoCert. As for the farm: approached by a winding road dotted with bungalows, it's an 18th-century house with wooden shutters and a newer gîte attached. But what will thrill you are the views, of vineyards exploding with biodiversity and a forested valley, wonderful from the multi-windowed sitting room and the sunlounged terrace. Inside all is breezy, modern, light: beige and cream tiled floors, white walls, white sofa, crisp pine table, bright bedrooms with wooden floors, big bathroom. Pick up your baguettes by bike (two are provided), help yourself to cherries, apricots, figs from the garden, take an organic picnic to the small oak forest, spot deer at dusk – and don't miss Saussignac's restaurant, walking distance from the farm. Lovely.

Price	€295–€550 per week. B&B €70 per night.
Rooms	Gîte for 4 (1 twin/double, 1 daybed for 2 in sitting room).
Meals	Breakfast €5. Restaurant 850m. Picnics available.
Closed	B&B only from October to May.
Directions	Directions on booking.

Ethical Collection: Environment; Food.
See page 211.

Price band: C

Seán & Caroline Feely
Château Haut Garrigue,
24240 Saussignac

Tel	+33 (0)5 53 22 72 71
Email	caroline@hautgarrigue.com
Web	www.hautgarrigue.com

Ecolodge des Chartrons

A many-splendoured delight: city-central and eco-friendly, with lovely materials and the warmth of simplicity. Your relaxed and friendly hosts have put their earth-saving principles to work – compromising neither the planet nor stylish comfort – stripping the wonderful wide floorboards, insulating with cork and wool, fitting solar water heating and sun pipes to hyper-modern shower rooms, treating guests to organic linen, and providing all-organic breakfasts. Bordeaux's eco-renovation luminary Véronique chairs 'eco meetings' for the community, passing on her good sense and her humour. At the bottom of this quiet road flows the Garonne where cafés, shops and galleries teem in converted warehouses (English wine merchants traded here 300 years ago) and a mirror fountain baffles the mind. Bordeaux's superb trams, running all over the city, are an easy and eco-friendly way to hop from St André's Gothic cathedral to the wine cellars and restaurants of Le Gran Théâtre. The city's newly cleaned churches sparkle, finally able to breathe air free of fumes. A city-stay as it should be: sustainable and special.

Price	€110–€130.
Rooms	4: 3 doubles, 1 triple.
Meals	Restaurant 100m.
Closed	Rarely.
Directions	On foot from cathedral: west on Cours d'Alsace & de Lorraine to river; left along quay 1.5km to Quai des Chartrons; Rue Raze on left. Road directions and parking information on booking.

Véronique Daudin
Ecolodge des Chartrons,
23 rue Raze, 33000 Bordeaux
Tel   +33 (0)5 56 81 49 13
Email   ecolodge33@free.fr
Web   www.ecolodgedeschartrons.com

Ethical Collection: Environment;
Community; Food.
See page 211.

Price band: D

Domaine des Faures

This impressive 17th-century manor house of creamy stone and dove-grey shutters is part of a bastide farm – an edifice built to repel attackers. There's nothing hostile about the Standens, who arrived from the UK in 2006 and have wrought wonders. The interior has been completely but sensitively renovated, with geothermal heating hidden beneath the venerable flagstones on the ground floor, and double glazing throughout. Roaring log fires keep you warm in winter, fans cool you in summer. Upstairs, wooden floors and smooth white walls give the bedrooms – one family room, three large doubles – a sense of unfussy calm. Each room has its own modern bathroom; only the 300-year-old stone flags hint at the house's history. New to farming, the Standens have an organic herd of Aubrac-Salers cattle grazing their 100 acres of rolling pasture. In the formal gardens, a geothermal saltwater pool is at your disposal all year. Rent the whole manor or stay as a B&B guest; classic French breakfasts of bread and organic jams are served at a circular glass table with black dining chairs, and in the garden in summer.

Price	€75-€90. Whole house (sleeps 9) €1,250-€2,500 per week.
Rooms	4: 3 doubles, 1 family room for 3. House available for self-catering.
Meals	Dinner with wine, €25. Restaurant 2km.
Closed	Never.
Directions	From Bergerac, signs to Issigeac, Villeréal & Monpazier. Right at wooden cross just before Monpazier on country road; Les Faures signed.

Ethical Collection: Environment; Food. See page 211.

Price band: C

Ray & Jacinta Standen
Domaine des Faures,
24540 Gaugeac

Tel   +33 (0)5 53 27 98 08
Email   raystanden@domainedesfaures.com
Web   www.domainedesfaures.com

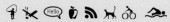

L'Auberge Les Liards

Cycling, hiking, horse riding and courses on African percussion: this is an active, invigorating place. International development workers Astrid and Walter have renovated the farm ruins – some are 15th-century – with impressive consideration for the environment. They've used wool insulation from the local organic farm, linseed oil finishes, solar-driven electrics, and natural textiles made by Russian monks. Passionate experts in eco construction, they have travelled the world and their experiences enliven the cuisine – especially on Monday nights, when everyone gathers together to eat at one big table. In the twin and double farmhouse rooms and the two 'family' barn spaces, the themes are minimalism, informality and naturalness. Wooden floors, plain stone and plaster walls, superb organic mattresses. No frills here, but magnificent vistas over the Auvergne volcanic chain and masses for outdoor adventurers. Catch your breath at those views from the four-bedded room with the terrace – and let the animals, open spaces and children's events keep the young ones supremely happy.

Price	€39–€76.
Rooms	4: 1 double, 1 twin, 1 quadruple, 1 family room for 5.
Meals	Dinner €18. Wine €13.
Closed	November–April.
Directions	From Sauxillanges, D39 towards Condat-lès-Montboissier; 1.5km after Sauxillanges, left dir. Egliseneuve des Liards (D705); follow signs to Auberge.

Astrid Ursem & Walter Verhoeve
L'Auberge Les Liards,
Lieu-dit Les Liards,
63490 Égliseneuve des Liards

Tel	+33 (0)4 73 96 89 44
Email	info@lesliards.com
Web	www.lesliards.com

Ethical Collection: Environment; Community; Food.
See page 211.

Price band: C

Château de Durianne

Since moving in five years ago, the Chambons have poured heart and soul into resuscitating this 500-year-old château; in the family for 200 years, it lay unloved for 100 of them. Now, full of portraits and antiques and 120-year-old wallpaper discovered in the attic (lovingly re-instated), it feels like home. Naturally fallen wood from the garden and the local sawmill heat both rooms and water (an ancient recipe of hot bricks in beds helps too!), a 19th-century rainwater harvesting system has been re-established and holds 10,000 litres, and sheep's wool and hemp insulate the attics. The one impressive B&B room (large, lofty, raftered and tiled) overlooks a farm where the Chambons keep hens and – soon to come – sheep. The as-yet uncultivated garden is long and grassy, the orchard is home to two donkeys and a pony who polish off all green waste (spare a thought for them as you savour your delicious organic breakfast and dinner!) and the village is just down the lane. The juice from the estate apples is superb and when friendly Madame is not too busy, she'll join you for coffee and a chat. *Minimum stay two nights.*

Price	€55. Whole castle (sleeps 6-9) €1,200 per week (June-August).
Rooms	1 family suite for 2-4. Castle available for self-catering.
Meals	Dinner with wine, €15. Restaurant 3km.
Closed	Never.
Directions	Le Puy en Velay D103 for Lavoute & Vorey 2km; right D103 to Durianne; in village, take the only right, unmarked; château 50m on left.

Ethical Collection: Environment; Food.
See page 211.

Price band: C

Françoise & Jean-Nicolas
Chambon du Garay
Château de Durianne,
43700 Le Monteil

Tel	+33 (0)4 71 02 90 36
Email	info@chateaudedurianne.com
Web	www.chateaudedurianne.com

Rose Art

An endearingly courteous and generous couple live here with all the time in the world for you and a delightful art gallery in their vaulted basement: Madame embroiders but shows other artists' work and their son produces good organic wines and eaux de vie. The family have eaten organically for almost 50 years and with their naturally painted house, chemical-free garden and eco-friendly cleaning products they've earned a hat tip from EcoCert. It's a rustic old wine merchant's house and the price reflects the décor, but the picturesque village, the rooms under the hemp-insulated roof, the lovely view of orchards and meadows, and the brook to sing you to sleep, all, after a fine meal with your adorable hosts, make it special. If homeopathy and medicinal plants/herbs are your thing, the family have used them for generations, so there's plenty to learn. And there's a laid-back garden with a playhouse for children, books galore – take your pick – and a piano anyone may play; golf is down the road. The setting is very lovely, and the lakes and mountains are close.

Price	From €50.
Rooms	2: 1 twin, 1 suite for 4-5.
Meals	Dinner €15. Wine €10-€12.
Closed	Rarely.
Directions	Lons le Saunier to Chalon; right before SNCF station onto D117 for Macornay; D41 to Vernantois; left before houses & follow signs.

	Monique & Michel Ryon
	Rose Art,
	8 rue Lacuzon,
	39570 Vernantois
Fax	+33 (0)3 84 47 17 28
Email	rose.art@wanadoo.fr

Ethical Collection: Environment; Food.
See page 211.

Price band: B

Entry 79   Map 2

Chalet Châtelet

The lush Vallée d'Abondance envelops this pretty new pine chalet, whose owners fizz with enthusiasm for the life they share with guests. There are oak floors, soft shapes, high ceilings, reclaimed furniture and works by Suzie's arty family. Pascal and Suzie built their home with the aim of living in utter comfort while having zero impact on the planet. Their mission was to integrate an eco house into the vernacular, orientate for the best views and maximise solar potential. Hand-chiselled local logs packed with lambs wool form one part; honeycomb bricks and local stone set in lime another. Warmth comes from a 'stone with soul' Finnish stove, clever insulation (that also includes cork and hemp) and solar panels (photovoltaic and thermal). Expect cultured chat in the intimate dining room, where Suzie serves organic meals cooked on the log-burning range. Produce is as local as can be. Wake from a deep sleep amidst soft organic linen to stunning views; shower with French natural soaps in dreamy bathrooms; gaze at mountains you plan to climb or ski that day. A home from home embraced by green. *Ask about ski & activity packages.*

Price	€90-€190.
Rooms	4: 2 doubles, 2 triples.
Meals	Dinner with wine, €30.
Closed	Rarely.
Directions	Thonon D902 for Morzine & Vallée d'Abondance. After 2nd tunnel, left at r'bout D22 for Vallée d'Abondance & Châtel. After La Solitude, right onto D32 Bonnevaux. At church fork left; chalet 300m on left.

Ethical Collection: Environment; Food.
See page 211.

Price band: E

Pascal & Suzie Immediato
Chalet Châtelet,
Route d'Abondance,
74360 Bonnevaux
Tel   +33 (0)4 50 73 69 48
Email   p.s.immediato@orange.fr
Web   www.chalet-chatelet.com

Maison Coutin

A year-round Alpine dream. In summer it's all flowers, birds and rushing streams, even a resident eagle. In winter you can ski or snow-walk across country. Or take the ski lift, 500m away, to the vast terrain of Les Arcs…Val d'Isère is not far. Delicious, mostly organic food is cooked in the wood oven here: there are four bio-vegetable gardens in the area and your plate is stacked with the fruits of their produce. The breakfast table displays jams from the garden's apples and pears, homemade breads, honeys and yogurt and eggs from the hens. The house has been superbly restored by young, friendly, dynamic host Franck, a mason who specialises in traditional techniques; walls are wrapped in wool, paints are 100% natural. Then there are the extras: solar panels heating hot water, wood pellets fuelling the biomass boiler. Your hosts cater well for children: yours can make friends with theirs, there are early suppers and Claude will babysit in the evening. Bedrooms are filled with views, there's a smallish comfortable day room with a handy fridge and an eco ethos that pervades the whole friendly place.

Price	€54–€60.
Rooms	3: 1 triple, 2 suites (1 for 4, 1 for 4–6).
Meals	Dinner with wine, €19. Children €6–€11. Restaurant 3km.
Closed	Rarely.
Directions	From Albertville N90 to Moutiers; on for Bourg St Maurice. Right onto D87E to Peisey Nancroix; left to Peisey centre; follow 3 green arrows; 9km from main road to house.

Claude Coutin & Franck Chenal
Maison Coutin,
73210 Peisey Nancroix

Tel	+33 (0)4 79 07 93 05
Email	maison-coutin@orange.fr
Web	www.maison-coutin.fr.st

Ethical Collection: Environment; Food.
See page 211.

Price band: C

Les Roudils

Breakfast among the butterflies – in one of the most idyllic places in France. High up in the nature-rich Monts d'Ardèche the views are inspiring and the peace supreme. The house, built of stone and wood from the chestnut forests, has been lovingly restored, so bedrooms are sunny, simple, rustic, authentic. Furniture-maker Gil crafts tables, staircases and doors from surrounding chestnut, elm, ash and olive, Marie is a member of 'Menus Curieux' and runs cookery courses extolling wild plants. Local produce is promoted and celebrated and breakfasts are entirely organic – poached eggs with paprika, pancakes with heather honey, seasonal fruits, dozens of jams. (Marie makes the heavenly apricot and rosemary preserves; Gil makes the aperitifs and chestnut, heather and raspberry honey.) Walls are limewashed, insulation is from sheep's wool, heating is solar helped by biomass, and all is composted and recycled. The garden exhibits ancient varieties of trees planted by your lovely hosts. Come for sunshine, music and warm hospitable people, at the end of the long winding road. Paradise!

Price	€60. Extra person €18.
Rooms	3: 2 doubles, 1 family suite for 5.
Meals	Restaurant 4km.
Closed	November–March.
Directions	From Aubenas, N102 for Le Puy; 8.5km. At Lalevade, left to Jaujac centre. By Café des Loisirs, over river & follow signs 4km along narrow mountain road.

Ethical Collection: Environment; Food.
See page 211.

Price band: C

Marie & Gil Florence
Les Roudils,
07380 Jaujac

Tel   +33 (0)4 75 93 21 11
Email le-rucher-des-roudils@wanadoo.fr
Web   www.lesroudils.com

Canvaschic

Yurts are in! And here is one of the first multi-yurt camps. Lodewijk and Ruth started with just three at their old site in Languedoc but (with two young children) have moved up in scale and location to the top of the beautiful Gorge d'Ardèche. On an old camping ground within a nature reserve, the new camp retains the air of communal living – there's an excellent shared toilet and shower block, and breakfast (fresh, local, delicious) is provided in the main building. Raised on wooden platforms, the yurts are scattered sparingly among leafy oak trees. Inside, each is about as chic as a tent can be: a large four-poster bed, a dressing table and two bedside lanterns to provide a soft evening glow. They are extraordinarily durable cocoons of comfort. The campsite is named 'milles étoiles' and the sensitive use of solar lanterns at night helps you count every single one of them. Rent a bike and explore the glorious forest gorges of the Ardèche; swim in the river; discover the beach at La Chataignerale; and on your return, sleep in style without leaving a harmful trace. Sheer delight.

Price	£255 (sterling) for 3 nights. From £595 for 1 week.
Rooms	14 yurts: 4 for 2, 10 for 4. Shared showers. 5 shared kitchens.
Meals	Breakfast €4-€6. Lunch/dinner €4-€10.
Closed	November-April.
Directions	4km from Labastide de Virac, road to Orgnac; left to Hameau des Crottes. Signed Milles Etoiles to track, camp 200m on left. Or train: TGV Paris-Avignon, then bus to Vagnas for pick-up.

Ethical Collection: Environment; Food. See page 211.

Price band: C

Ruth Lawson
Canvaschic,
Milles Etoiles, Camping du Mas de Serret,
07150 Labastide de Virac

Tel	+33 (0)4 75 38 42 77 (campsite)
Email	info@canvaschic.com
Web	www.canvaschic.com

Mas de la Bousquette – Le Grenier & Le Mûrier

Wildlife and flowers flourish in the meadows of waving grass, birds nest in the walls. The ancient, rose-roofed mas rests at the foot of castle-topped Lussan. The countryside rolls out before you, the air is pure and the sun is golden – even in winter. In two towers, one where silkworms were once reared, are two charming gîtes linked by a roofed terrace: expect muslin curtains, comfortable beds, a beautifully equipped kitchen. Heating is part geothermal, lights low energy, soaps local, and the land is wildlife-rich and chemical-free. Pippa and Tim are generous people and offer you books, games, bicycles, binoculars, fresh fruit, lavender, fresh bread at your door, towels for the heat-pump-warmed pool. Pippa loves cooking, gives children organic cookery lessons and you a free dinner on arrival, and runs a shop selling a range of organics. This is southern France at its most peaceful, within walking distance of a restaurant and near lovely Uzès. The garden is big, with a willow tree beside a pond, hammocks and lazy chairs; there's an old orchard too – peg out your washing among peacocks and rare-breed chickens.

Price	Le Grenier €780–€1,600.
	Le Mûrier €550–€1,200.
	Prices per week.
Rooms	Le Grenier sleeps 4–6.
	Le Mûrier sleeps 2–4.
Meals	Dinner with wine €37.50.
	Restaurant 500m.
Closed	Never.
Directions	Directions on booking.

Ethical Collection: Environment; Food.
See page 211.

Price band: D

Tim & Pippa Forster
Mas de la Bousquette
– Le Grenier & Le Mûrier,
30580 Lussan
Tel   +33 (0)4 66 72 71 60
Email   masbousquette@free.fr
Web   www.mas-bousquette.com

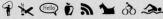

L'Orri de Planès

High on the hill, at 1,600m, a huge old barn of Pyrenean stone renovated with the future of the planet in mind. Arif and Marta are self-confessed ecologists and their lodge is one of our greenest. Even in winter, when deep snow allows snowshoeing or cross-country skiing from the door, sunshine is the key to sustainability. Evergreen solar is captured for heating and electricity, locked in by argon-filled glass panes. The spring-rain-filled pool is panel-powered too; excess energy is sold to others. The no-frills lodge, with its vast wooden beams, is built entirely with local materials and says "less is more". The superb position, on the Cardagne plain between two hiker-friendly mountain ranges, adds intricacy to the experience – and what an experience! Look north to France and south to Spain; spring flourishes with wildflowers, butterflies swoon around them. For breakfast and supper, you are fed, beautifully, at long wooden tables on local and/or organic everything: pâtés and cheeses, meats, yogurts, charcuterie, honey, wine. Arif and Marta are pioneers in eco tourism and memories of their lodge will last forever.

Price	€30 p.p. Children €25. Half board €35-€50.
Rooms	10: 1 family room for 4; 4 doubles, 4 twins, sharing 4 baths; dorm for 6-8 with bath, shower & kitchen.
Meals	Dinner with wine, €20. Children €10.
Closed	3 weeks in May. 3 weeks in November.
Directions	From Perpignan N116 for Prades; at Mont Louis, D32 to La Cabanasse, St Pierre des Forçats & Planès (5km from Mont Louis). Signed from town. Or train; 15-minute walk from station.

Arif Qureshi & Marta Maristany
L'Orri de Planès,
Trailside Eco-Lodge,
Cases de Mitg, 66210 Planès

Tel	+33 (0)4 68 04 29 47
Email	contact@orrideplanes.com
Web	www.orrideplanes.com

Ethical Collection: Environment;
Community; Food.
See page 211.

Price band: B

Entry 85   Map 2

Le Camp

Discover the thrill of sleeping under canvas, encounter nature in style. You could be in deepest Africa but you're in south west France – on a hillside surrounded by oaks, birds and butterflies, with a delicious pool cleansed by gravel and plants. Stephen and Sally are young, enthusiastic, deeply committed to the planet and happy to share their dream. They sourced the tents in Africa, then filled them with big beds, fine linen, soft solar lighting and pretty throws; lazy chairs and cushions, too. The kitchen and dining areas are spacious and superb (Sally has thought of everything, from pots and pans to spices and oil) so dinners resemble one big house party... there are lots of quiet corners for intimate dining and a big fire pit to cosy up to. The huge two-bedroom tents (on decks made from sustainable timber) and the romantic yurts (with removable roof caps so you can wonder at the stars) are set well apart. In the indoor/outdoor shower house the water is recycled, the soaps are local and organic and the composting loos were sourced in Sweden. No cars, no rules, just green heaven for all ages. *Minimum 4-7 nights in summer.*

Price	€145–€195 per night for 2.
Rooms	5 tents: 3 for 2-5 with wc; 2 for 2 + child. Showers & wcs in separate block.
Meals	Breakfast included. Shared kitchen. Restaurant 5km.
Closed	October-April.
Directions	From St Antonin Noble Val, D115 towards Varen & Laguepie. After 11km, D33 towards Verfeil. At war memorial in Arnac, left. Up hill for 1km, on right. Or train to Lexos.

Ethical Collection: Environment; Community. See page 211.

Price band: E

Sally O'Hare
Le Camp,
82330 Varen

Tel	+33 (0)5 63 65 48 34
Email	info@lecamp.co.uk
Web	www.lecamp.co.uk

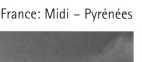

Ferme de Técouère

The night skies are aglow with stars and peace, here in the gentle wooded countryside of southern France. You'll get a lovely welcome from this young, humorous, generous French family living The Good Life at the foot of the Pyrenees. They have renovated their 1930s farmhouse, turned the connecting barn into a gîte, decorated with natural paints, installed geothermal heating for warm floors and added solar panels for hot water. With a plant nursery and a potager it's a foodie's delight; and interesting for children too, thanks to a tribe of flop-eared rabbits, hens and geese, and the fine pool with view to the Pyrenees on a clear day. Your gîte has new terracotta tiles, pale-gold stone walls and a feastful of beams, squashy sofas round the fire, an armoire of games, a kitchen with mod cons. Rustic bedrooms lie at the top of some fairly steep stairs (stair gate in place), their pretty antique beds inviting with new mattresses and white laundered linen. Book in for table d'hôtes if you can: you may be treated to duck cooked over an open fire, and a glass of bitter-sweet armagnac before bed.

Price	€400–€980 per week. B&B option €65.
Rooms	Gite for 5 (1 double, 1 triple).
Meals	Dinner with wine, €19. By arrangement.
Closed	January & February.
Directions	From Maubourguet, D943 dir. Auch & Marciac. On outskirts of town, D50 dir. Sauveterre & Saint-Justin. At Sauveterre, after intersection, 2nd left, then left again. House up the hill.

Françoise & Patrice Pawlak
Ferme de Técouère,
65700 Sauveterre
Tel   +33 (0)5 62 96 32 62
Email   tecouere.pawlak@wanadoo.fr

Ethical Collection: Environment; Food.
See page 211.

Price band: C

Entry 87   Map 2

Mas de la Rabassière

Fanfares of lilies at the door, Haydn inside and Michael smiling in his chef's apron. Rabassière means 'where truffles are found' and the epicurean dinners are a treat. Wines from the neighbouring vineyard grace the terrace table – along with a sculpted dancer. Rail station pick-ups, cookery classes using home-produced olive oil and jogging companionship are all part of your host's unflagging hospitality – with the help of Thévi, his calm Singaporean assistant. Michael was posted to France by a multi-national, fell in love with the country, and on retirement slipped into this unusually lush corner of Provence. Books, conversation, a piano (in tune!) – such a friendly house. Michael offers a fair pricing policy to single people and those with children and is switched on to sustainability: he works locally with the green mayoral candidate, and has introduced solar thermals, insulation, heat exchangers and wood-burning stoves to his Provençal antiques and English country-house style. Come savour this charmingly generous house and enjoy homemade croissants with fig jam under the wisteria-covered veranda.

Price	€130. Singles €80.
Rooms	2 doubles.
Meals	Dinner with wine, €45.
Closed	Rarely.
Directions	A54 exit 13 to Grans on D19; right on D16 to St Chamas; just before r'way bridge, left for Cornillon & up hill 2km; house on right before tennis court. Map sent on request.

Ethical Collection: Environment; Food.
See page 211.

Price band: D

Michael Frost
Mas de la Rabassière,
Route de Cornillon,
13250 Saint Chamas

Tel	+33 (0)4 90 50 70 40
Email	michaelfrost@rabassiere.com
Web	www.rabassiere.com

Domaine de la Blaque

Caroline and Jean-Luc, organic agriculturalists for 20 years, make fascinating hosts; theirs was one of the first properties in the Var to be classified 'eco'. Their vision of sustainable construction has been woven into the restoration using a mixture of local stone and wood, natural paints and insulation from hemp and natural renders. Solar seductively heats your hot water, rainwater is harvested so as to not waste a drop and you are surrounded by nature at its best. These lovely hosts have that artistic flair that puts the right things together naturally: palest pink-limed walls with white linen; old-stone courtyard walls with massed jasmine and honeysuckle; yoga groups and painters with wide open skies. Caroline is a photographer and Jean-Luc is passionate about astronomy and teaches introductory courses in his observatory – the stars shine brightly here, away from civilisation. They also produce olives, truffles and timber, and love sharing their remote estate with like-minded travellers. Each pretty, independent ground-floor bedroom has a kitchenette and its own little terrace.

Price	€70–€80.
Rooms	2: 1 double, 1 twin, each with kitchenette.
Meals	Restaurants 5km.
Closed	Rarely.
Directions	A8 exit St Maximum; D560 before Barjols; at Brue-Auriac D35 to Varages; sign on left leaving village for Tavernes; follow signs, dirt track part of way.

Caroline & Jean-Luc Plouvier
Domaine de la Blaque,
83670 Varages
Tel   +33 (0)4 94 77 86 91
Email   ploublaque@hotmail.com
Web   www.lablaque.com

Ethical Collection: Environment.
See page 211.

Price band: C

Une Campagne en Provence

Water gushes and flows throughout the 170-acre estate, springtime's streams abound. In the 12th century the Knights Templar created a myriad of irrigation channels for the water. In the 21st century, the Fussler family have found the holy grail of water self-sufficiency: anaerobic composting, reed ponds, degreasing systems. This stunning bastide keeps its massive fortress-like proportions and bags of character. The main house is arranged around a central patio; stairs lead up to the bedrooms. Simple Provençal furnishings are lit by huge windows, floors are *terre cuite*, there are cosy 'boutis' quilts and sumptuous towels, and bathrooms are cleverly worked around original features. Underfloor heating is powered by a ground-source pump. The well-stocked apartments have knockout views across fields fostering biodiversity: wild fruits and 60 species of butterfly. Claude is renowned for his knowledge of sustainable development so his library is worth a ponder. Restive teenagers can relax in the media room, others the Turkish bath or outdoor pool. An isolated paradise for Templar enthusiasts.

Price	€90–€120.
	Apartments €600–€910 per week.
Rooms	4 + 4: 3 doubles, 1 studio for 2 (without kitchen). 3 apartments for 4, 1 studio for 2.
Meals	Breakfast included for self-caterers. Hosted dinner with wine, €32. Restaurant 7km.
Closed	January & February.
Directions	A8 Aix-Nice exit St Maximin la Ste Baume; then D28 to Bras. After 9km, follow signs.

Ethical Collection: Environment; Food. See page 211.

Price band: D

Monsieur & Madame Fussler
Une Campagne en Provence,
Domaine le Peyrourier,
83149 Bras

Tel	+33 (0)4 98 05 10 20
Email	info@provence4u.com
Web	www.provence4u.com

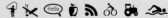

Eco Hotel Cristallina

Chunky stone paths lead to traditional Ticinese villages, where granite houses perch high in lush chestnut-forested mountains among ravines, waterfalls and clear waters – the Maggia provides a soothing setting for a healthy holiday. In season, the Swiss come to enjoy simplicity in Coglio's beautifully restored houses – though the Vallemaggia Magic Blues Festival is another pull. Marco is proud of his eco hotel and you see why: it is carbon-neutral, nothing is wasted, walls and ceilings are insulated, there are measuring systems to reduce water use and recycling cupboards on every floor. The old building has been restored and a new wing built with the help of a specialist architect, complete with 20 solar panels to soak up every last drop of sunshine; it's all so efficient that any surplus energy is donated to the community. There's a woodchip boiler, too. Clean, crisp, wood-scented rooms have beds wrapped in cool organic cotton, most ingredients are home-grown and organic, vegetarians are looked after beautifully and you can eat looking onto open fields while children play on swings. Idyllic.

Price	CHF 100-CHF 200 (€66-€132).
Rooms	13: 5 doubles sharing bath; 6 doubles, 1 triple, 1 family room for 4.
Meals	Lunch from €10. Dinner from €25. Wine from €14.
Closed	6 Jan-27 Feb; last 2 weeks November.
Directions	Locarno-Vallemaggia dir. Maggiatal & Centovalli; at Ponte Brolla dir. Maggia & Coglio. Signed. Or, train to Locarno, then bus to Maggiatal, stop at Coglio. Hotel 300m, signed.

Marco & Tamara Kälin-Medici
Eco Hotel Cristallina,
6678 Coglio,
Vallemaggia

Tel	+41 (0)91 753 11 41
Email	info@hotel-cristallina.ch
Web	www.hotel-cristallina.ch

Ethical Collection: Environment; Community; Food.
See page 211.

Price band: D

Entry 91   Map 3

Ca' Stella

The wealthy local who built this beautiful stone house in 1546 chose a plum site. Two icy mountain rivers converge behind it, a quiet, sunny piazza lies before it. Vegetarian owner Helia Blocher sees the guest house as her life's work. She bought it in 1998, restoring it as greenly as the local historic society allowed. Isoflock insulation backed up by a biomass boiler keeps out the Alpine night's chill; water in the shared modern bathrooms is solar-heated. Many of the sun-drenched bedrooms have original painted ceilings, all are comfortably furnished, with organic sheets and towels. Large groups get the snug attic dorm room. Breakfast is a feast of local organic fare, with fruit and veg from Helia's organic garden. Order other meals on booking, or cook for yourself in the stone-flagged kitchen – Helia and her friendly staff will point you to the organic supermarket. Don't feel guilty about waste, lucky local pigs get the leftovers. The comfy recreation room, strewn with cushions, lined with books, has beautiful mountain views from the balcony. Unwind.
Self-catering house in village also available.

Price	CHF 95-CHF 140. Dormitory from CHF 25 p.p.
Rooms	8: 2 doubles, 2 twins, 2 triples, 1 quadruple, 1 dorm for 12. Some bathrooms shared.
Meals	Breakfast CHF 10. Guest kitchen. Restaurants nearby.
Closed	Mid-November to mid-March.
Directions	From Locarno dir. Vallemaggia to Bignasco. 1st right signed Schwimmbad; 1st left, 100m to hotel. Or, train to Locarno & bus to Bignasco. 200m walk from stop.

Ethical Collection: Environment.
See page 211.

Price band: C

Mrs Helia Blocher
Ca' Stella,
6676 Bignasco,
Vallemaggia

Tel	+41 (0)91 754 34 34
Email	info@ca-stella.ch
Web	www.ca-stella.ch

Eco Hotel Locanda del Giglio

Long walks in glorious mountains await you, but an electric buggy collects you on arrival, from the steep, sweet village. The epitome of modern eco design, this hotel was built in 2005, when owner Fausto pitched in with local craftsmen to create a green hideaway on the forest fringes. A winding path leads to a scented wildflower and herb garden, a tipi and terraces. A small wellness centre is to come. The sun generates electricity and hot water, top-grade insulation means there's no need for heating (but note the woodchip furnace just in case) and water comes from a mountain spring. The supply is weather dependent, so guests get tips on how to save – tricky, since shower rooms flaunt eco treats. Vibrant Indian and Tibetan rugs and bedspreads add colour to pale wood furniture in pine-scented bedrooms, and each room has a balcony for those breathtaking views. Eating-in does the planet a favour – Fausto and Mina are members of Slow Food, and almost everything, wine included, is local, seasonal and organic... the restaurant also specialises in vegan and vegetarian. A small hotel with a big heart.

Price	CHF 80-CHF 150.
Rooms	7: 3 doubles, 2 bunk suites for 6; 1 double, 1 bunk room for 6 sharing shower.
Meals	Dinner from CHF 12. Wine from CHF 26. (Not Tuesday.)
Closed	7 January-February.
Directions	Zurich E35 exit Lugano Nord. Via Cantonala, signed Roveredo C. Park on left. Electric buggy pick up. Or, train Zurich-Lugano & bus Val Colla & Tesserete; stop Roveredo C; 100m to hotel.

Fausto Foletti & Mina Bamert
Eco Hotel Locanda del Giglio,
6957 Roveredo Capriasca,
Lugano

Tel	+41 (0)91 930 09 33
Email	locandadelgiglio@hotmail.com
Web	www.locandadelgiglio.ch

Ethical Collection: Environment; Food.
See page 211.

Price band: C

Ecogîte du Charron

The former wheelwright's workshop is surrounded by a gentle Swiss landscape on the edge of the village. Now it holds two modest gîtes. Grassy, flowery outdoor spaces have picnic tables alongside the (peaceful) road; shared with the owners is their child-friendly garden, with sandpit and playhouse, hammock and swings, and ponies, Bleu-Ciel and Panache. The Benoits are a very gentle and engaging couple with three young children who are acting on their green principles, from the harvesting of rainwater to the photovoltaic panels. They keep hens, too, and make syrups and jams from pears, cherries, quinces and plums – delicious – and wine from their vines. The apartments are light, lofty, spotless and full of modern pine; mezzanine floors create sleeping spaces and the bigger (better) gîte has a sofabed downstairs. Shower rooms are tiny and kitchens basic so Tania's pizzas and pies (homemade and fresh from the wood oven) are worth ordering in advance. It's a flat but pretty region – bring the bikes and follow the canals. In summer there are the rivers to brave – and a big outdoor pool in Orbe. Lovely.

Price	CHF 380–CHF 800 per week.
Rooms	2 gîtes: 1 for 2, 1 for 2-4.
Meals	Restaurants within walking distance.
Closed	Never.
Directions	Lausanne-Neuchâtel exit Chavornay. At village r'bout, left. Follow Grand'Rue for 300m. Or, by train to Chavornay.

Ethical Collection: Environment.
See page 211.

Price band: C

Famille Yves Benoit
Ecogîte du Charron,
Grand'Rue 69,
CH-1373 Chavornay, Orbe

Tel	+41 (0)24 441 09 43
Email	demande@charron.ch
Web	www.hotes.ch

Hotel Balance

Remember Heidi's bedroom in her grandfather's house – wooden floor, walls and ceiling, wooden bed with snug white quilt, sun streaming through the shutters? That's what this Alpine hotel brings to mind – just add a dose of eco tweakery. Hands-on owner Roland's dedication – here and in the community – has earned a full Ibex rating for sustainability. Food is 100% organic, and vegetarian. Isoflock insulation makes the most of the geothermal heating. Water is solar heated, photovoltaic panels produce electricity. Bathrooms have showers not baths, to conserve water. And the breathtaking mountain setting is enhanced by an Alpine meadow garden, planted with fragrant herbs used by the kitchen to make teas; benches hide in nooks and crannies, children romp in the play area. The outdoor 'bio-pool' uses no chemicals and its water is warmed by the sun, and cleaned by filtration. Shiatsu and ayurveda massage, yoga classes and a meditation room eliminate stress. Five apartments in the 'wasserschloss' in the grounds echo these high standards – and have extra space and privacy. *Minimum stay four nights in apartments.*

Price	CHF 270. Apartments from CHF 175 for 2.
Rooms	22 + 7: 22 twins/doubles (sharing shower rooms). 7 apartments for 2-4.
Meals	Dinner, 5 courses, CHF 40-CHF 50. Wine CHF 40.
Closed	Rarely.
Directions	From Martigny, follow mountain road to Les Granges. Or, train to Martigny & mountain train to Les Marécottes.

	Family Schatzmann-Eberle
	Hotel Balance,
	1922 Les Granges, Veveyse
Tel	+41 (0)27 761 15 22
Email	info@vegetarisches-hotel.ch
Web	www.vegetarisches-hotel.ch

Ethical Collection: Environment; Food. See page 211.

Price band: E

Entry 95   Map 3

Éco-Hôtel L'Aubier

If you fret about food miles, and ponder the provenance of your pud, this is the hotel for you. Bread and preserves are made in the kitchen. Milk, six kinds of cheese, yogurt, cream, fruit, veg, beef, veal and pork come from the biodynamic farm next door. Crops and animals are raised organically, according to the astronomical calendar; if you're here at the right time you can help sow next year's wheat. The farm, farm shop, restaurant and hotel are owned and run by a charitable foundation dedicated to sustainable living while the hotel has the 5-Ibex award for sustainability, the highest possible rating. The main building is a traditional Swiss mountain hotel – a steeply pitched roof, dormer windows peeping through it, white stone walls, and shutters and wooden balconies with views over wildflower meadows, mountains and lakes. Bedrooms are pleasingly modern, light and airy. Ten rooms were added in 2000 in the form of modular wooden eco cabins on stilts, with jaw-dropping Alpine views. After a day in the fresh mountain air, what could be better than a sumptuous meal with impeccable credentials?

Price	CHF 160-CHF 210.
Rooms	25: 13 twin/doubles, 10 singles, 2 family rooms for 4-5.
Meals	Dinner from CHF 18. Wine CHF 20.
Closed	2 weeks in January.
Directions	From Neuchâtel, follow signs to Pontarlier. At the first forest after Corcelles, right signed Montezillon.

Ethical Collection: Environment; Food.
See page 211.

Price band: D

Marc Desaules
Éco-Hôtel L'Aubier,
Les Murailles 5,
2037 Montezillon, Neuchâtel
Tel   +41 (0)32 732 22 11
Email   contact@aubier.ch
Web   www.aubier.ch

L'Aubier: Le Café-Hôtel

A gem in Neuchâtel's old town, a maze of steep cobbled alleys, ancient houses and fountained squares. Run by the same charitable green foundation as its rural namesake Éco-Hôtel L'Aubier, this gorgeous old townhouse combines comfortable modern hotel with irresistible organic café. From pine-topped tables and white bentwood chairs you taste the delicious fruits of L'Aubier's biodynamic farm at Montezillon; they've won a 'Gout Mieux' award in recognition of their local, organic and seasonal food. Bask in sunshine on the first-floor terrace and order a freshly roasted and ground biodynamic coffee; treat yourself to something from a glorious array of baked goods, cheeses and salads. In contrast to the building's traditional exterior, the compact bedrooms are stylishly minimalist and painted in warm natural hues, with comfortable new beds and pale wood shelving. Three have small but perfectly formed bathrooms, the rest share a couple of showers and loos. The best of Neuchâtel lies at your feet; the 12th-century castle and venerable early-Gothic church are a step away.

Price	CHF 110–CHF 180.
Rooms	9: 3 doubles; 6 doubles sharing showers.
Meals	Breakfast from CHF 7. Lunch from CHF 10. Restaurants nearby.
Closed	Rarely.
Directions	5-minute walk from multi-storey parking Seyon or Pury in centre. Or, by train to Neuchâtel & bus to old town centre (1-min walk from bus stop Croiz-du-Marché; 3 mins from Place Pury).

Marc Desaules
L'Aubier: Le Café-Hôtel,
Rue du Château,
Place du Banneret, 2000 Neuchâtel

Tel	+41 (0)32 710 18 58
Email	lecafe@aubier.ch
Web	www.aubier.ch

Ethical Collection: Food.
See page 211.

Price band: D

Hotel Kürschner

Lots of packaged breaks to choose from here, with the emphasis on outdoor activities, wellness and diet. Treatments range from 'Fat Burn Specials' (fitness training and whole-body peelings) to 'Teeny Beauty' for young girls (back massages, facials and honey-vanilla baths) – you'll all go home glowing! The setting is Alpine-gorgeous, overlooking large lovely manicured grounds and the meadows and forests of the Gailtal (those well-cut meadows providing the hay for the spa's hay baths). The pool links indoors with outdoors, slatted wooden hammocks hang in the orchard, comfy plastic loungers flank the pool and there's masses for families to do: trips to the farm with ponies to ride, winter walks with sledges and lanterns. Inside, wooden furniture is treated with beeswax, floors are carpeted in wool, loos are low-flush and the water comes from their own springs. As is often the case in Austria, the meadows and the gardens are organically cultivated, so the food is wholesome and the vegetable juices home-produced. Bedrooms are large and traditional, with organic linen, retro furniture, floor-length drapes and several mod cons.

Price	€138–€194. Half-board €69–€96 p.p.
Rooms	35: 11 doubles, 8 singles, 16 suites for 2-5.
Meals	Dinner available. Wine from €12. Free lunch buffet every other day.
Closed	November-December.
Directions	From Salzburg A10 dir. Villach, exit to Lendorf dir. Lienz until Oberdrauburg. At Oberdrauburg follow signs to Kötschach. At Kötschach, right before church, up narrow lane.

Ethical Collection: Environment; Food.
See page 211.

Price band: E

Barbara Klauß
Hotel Kürschner,
Schlanke Gasse 74,
9640 Kötschach-Mauthen, Imst

Tel	+43 (0)4715 259
Email	info@hotel-kuerschner.at
Web	www.hotel-kuerschner.at

Gralhof

Wooden skiffs bob in the boathouse and the lake laps at the garden's feet. This exquisite wooden farmhouse in 80 hectares of woodland and lush cow-grazed pastures has been in the family for 500 years; in 1992 they went fully organic. Now the Knallers have opened their doors to those in search of peace, nature and beautiful food. Produce comes from local farms, coffees are fairtrade, breads are homemade and breakfasts are consumed at leisure – under the pear tree in summer and until 11am if you like. Dinners includes two menus, one of which is vegetarian, while the food is matched by the wines – Austrian, naturally. Two generations run a happy ship and whoever is in charge of the interiors has an excellent eye: all is simple but stylish, cosy but sophisticated. The trees from the forest line walls and floors and feed boiler and sauna, some rooms are insulated with reeds from the shore and there's a lovely old fireplace round which everyone gathers for drinks each night. In winter, the lake freezes to become Europe's largest ice rink; in summer, you can row on it, cycle round it – or brave a swim! Fabulous.

Price	€92–€130. Half-board (winter only) €70–€85 p.p.
Rooms	17: 14 doubles, 3 family rooms for 3–5.
Meals	Dinner from €8. Wine from €16.
Closed	15 October–25 December; 1 April–20 May.
Directions	Directions on booking.

Herr Knaller
Gralhof,
Neusach 7, 9762 Weissensee,
Spittal an der Drau
Tel   +43 (0)4713 2213
Email   info@gralhof.at
Web   www.gralhof.at

Ethical Collection: Environment; Community; Food.
See page 211.

Price band: D

Entry 99   Map 4

Bio Arche Hotel

Austria's "first eco hotel" (constructed from eco-treated woods, painted without chemicals, insulated with coconut fibre) is a striking take on a traditional country house. Three generations run this together, an engaging family who love having young ones to stay, so there are swings and sandpits in the garden and an attic full of toys. Water is solar-heated, sleeping areas are radi-aesthetically arranged, the herbal spa revitalises you and the meals are both vegetarian and 100% organic, with the waste going to the animals on the relatives' farm nearby (hens, horses, cows). Bedrooms are not stylish but light, airy, natural and cosy, our favourites the family 'bio-nests' under the steep pitched roofs. Bed linen is dried in the oxygen-rich air, floors are of wood or linoleum and the sun terrace has a stunning panorama. Delicious food is washed down with delicious Austrian wine and you could live off the breakfasts alone: a fine start for hikers and skiers. Health-orientated talks and activities abound (even snowball fights win prizes), there are torchlit cave walks close by and coach rides with Noric horses.

Price	€98–€108. Singles €50–€54. Family room €162–€186. Family apts from €108 for 2. All prices half-board. House from €85 p.n.
Rooms	16 + 1: 10 twins/doubles, 1 family room, 2 singles, 3 family apts (with kitchenette). House for 4.
Meals	Half-board only (except for house). Dinner from €12.
Closed	Two weeks in December.
Directions	Salzburg A10 to Villach; A2 dir. Klagenfurt; motorway St Veit/Glan dir. Brückl. At Brückl r'bout dir. Eberstein. At Eberstein dir. St Oswald. Signed.

Ethical Collection: Environment;
Community; Food.
See page 211.

Price band: C

Family Tessmann
Bio Arche Hotel,
St Oswald 70, 9372 Eberstein,
Sankt Veit an der Glan
Tel   +43 (0)4264 8120
Email   bio.arche@hotel.at
Web   www.bio.arche.hotel.at

Haus Troth

You are in a small, typically Austrian town, but mountain pastures, valley meadows and glassy lakes are a short walk from the front door. In this squeaky-green B&B, food is taken seriously: it is delicious, seasonal and totally organic. This energetic, committed English family make their own bacon, pâtés (fish and meat), jams from garden fruits, cakes and bread – even the ice creams are homemade. Bedrooms are light, airy and simple, with good mountain views, wooden furniture and pretty hand-printed fabrics from India; bed linen is Soil Association certified and soaps are organic. You are kept cosy with a biomass boiler and your solar-heated water is piping hot. The friendly Troths – "eco pacifists not eco warriors" – have moved to the right place: this region of Austria is 40% organic. They're also full of good suggestions for places to eat, lakes for swimming, walks and cycle rides galore, and can send you off with an organic packed lunch. The small garden is safe for children to play in, and makes a cool spot for a sundowner after a hard day's tobogganing – in winter *and* summer!

Price	£42-£46 (sterling).
Rooms	2: 1 double, 1 twin/double sharing shower. Rooms can interconnect.
Meals	Packed lunch €5. Restaurant 50m.
Closed	Never.
Directions	From Lofer (Germany) B311. From Saalfelden straight over r'bout; left at 2nd r'bout (3rd exit). House 150m on right. Or, by train to Saalfelden; 800m, opposite travel agent. 200m from bus station.

Jonathan & Dianne Troth
Haus Troth,
Bahnhofstrasse 23,
5760 Saalfelden, Salzburg

Tel	+43 (0)6582 7078 5
Email	lightgreen@aon.at
Web	www.lightgreen.co.uk

Ethical Collection: Environment; Food.
See page 211.

Price band: B

Grafenast

The red hall is graced by two antique buddhas, the pool went solar 35 years ago and the kitchen is 100% biodynamic: all produce is planted and harvested to the rhythms of the moon. That's how green Grafenast is. This supremely serene hotel has been in the family for a hundred years and offers something very special: the moment you arrive you sense it. The inspirational Unterlechner family are environmental campaigners and ethical employers who love their guests too and put on convivial dinners twice weekly – huge fun. As for the house, it's grown gracefully with the years and it charms all who stay, with its pale wood-panelled interiors and views that stretch to Innsbruck. The garden with tipi, terrace and treehouse nurtures over 70 herbs (Grandfather gives tours once a week in German) and only the best ingredients find their way to the kitchen – with truly delicious results. Bedrooms are beautiful, TV-free and overlook that enticing valley; beds are luxurious; pillows are filled with grain (comfy!). Swim in springwater in summer, sledge by torchlight in winter – it's bliss. *Ski museum, spa & creative courses.*

Price	€162. Full-board €344.
Rooms	23: 12 doubles, 7 singles, 4 suites.
Meals	Lunch €18-€26. Dinner €26-€36. Wine from €20.
Closed	November to mid-December; April to mid-May.
Directions	From Innsbruck exit Schwaz. Follow signs to Pillberg; 10km. Or, by train to Schwaz & bus 8 to hotel.

Ethical Collection: Environment; Community; Food. See page 211.

Price band: D

Dr Hansjörg & Marianne Unterlechner
Grafenast,
Pillbergstrasse 205,
6130 Schwaz

Tel	+43 (0)5242 63209
Email	peter@grafenast.at
Web	www.grafenast.at

Hof Klostersee

Impossible for you – or your children – to leave this haven without feeling revitalised: body and soul. Hof Klostersee is a biodynamic farm where everything grown and sold is caressed, naturally. Cheese has 24-hour attention, milking cows are fed organically, plants are strengthened from seed to avoid insect invaders. The farm is community-led — and what a happy bunch they are, from students learning biodynamics to elders given a home in a converted barn; even the goats smile as you greet them. Self-catering has never been so fulfilling. The farm shop stocks biodynamic *everything* and there's so much to do. Meet Gerlinde in her 'office' (the bakery) or her Italian partner Alberto in his (the mill); borrow bikes and cycle to the beach; feed the animals. The family apartments in the old workers' cottages have a large shared garden (the best and most fun are open-plan on the top floor) and the old hen house has been converted into a cosy country cottage with views onto a magnificent 500-year oak that shelters crocuses in spring. Gerlinde offers Steiner wellness for the mind, and there's shiatsu and massage available too.

Price	€40–€55 for 2; €50–€75 for 4. Prices per night.
Rooms	5 apartments for 2-4.
Meals	Occasional buffet, €11. Restaurant 700m.
Closed	Never.
Directions	Signed from Cismar. Or, by train to Oldenburg in Holstein or Neustadt in Holstein; bus to Grönwohldshorst.

Gerlinde Naegel
Hof Klostersee,
23743 Cismar-Grönwohldshorst

Tel	+49 (0)4366 517
Email	klostersee@gmx.de
Web	www.hof-klostersee.de

Ethical Collection: Environment; Community; Food.
See page 211.

Price band: C

Gut Netzow

Come in spring for the migrating birds, in autumn for the trees, in summer for the swimming. Five glacial lakes converge here like the fingers of a hand and the pine forests are thick with wildlife. Before the Michels bought the farmstead with all its outbuildings and space it was part of a huge East German collective; now it's heaven for young families and all who love the outdoors. There's a sand box and toys, football in the yard, table tennis in the stable. The apartments are spacious, not stylish but comfortable nonetheless, with pine furniture and wood-burners. Borrow a row boat or canoe and set off from the jetty, or take a bike out for the day – there are several provided. For cyclists it's paradise, with endless miles of tracks through pine and beech forests. Bird lovers too are in clover: cranes and ospreys are common, storks are not unusual, the cockerel crows and the cranes trumpet when migrating. The cows are organically reared, the hens range freely (children may collect eggs) and the dogs romp. The village is no beauty but nearby Templin is an architectural gem. *Minimum stay two nights.*

Price	€65-€125 for 2-6. Prices per night.
Rooms	Granary sleeps 6. Stable sleeps 6. Smithy sleeps 4.
Meals	Restaurants 8km.
Closed	Never.
Directions	Directions on booking.

Ethical Collection: Food.
See page 211.

Price band: B

Anna & Franz Christoph Michel
Gut Netzow,
Gut Netzow 1,
17268 Templin

Tel	+49 (0)3987 3029
Email	mail@gutnetzow.de
Web	www.gutnetzow.de

Ökotel Hamburg

A quiet leafy suburb of Hamburg is the last place you'd expect to find a cutting-edge hotel. Built in 1996 as a pioneering eco project, it ticks all the boxes: triple glazing, efficient lighting, solar panels, green roofing, recycled-paper insulation, loos flushed with rainwater. The furniture was made from sustainable timber, leaving a lovely woody smell; the murals of indigenous trees were painted by a local artist – this is more Alpine chalet than city hotel. Bedrooms are pleasingly simple, with whitewashed walls, oiled wood floors, hand-crafted pieces and large balconies overlooking leafy streets. Sheets and towels are organic, blankets and carpets are of untreated wool; minibar offerings are all-organic, too. When you're not in your room, rest assured it'll be cleaned in an environmentally friendly way, and anything you've thrown away, sorted for recycling. Dinner is certified 100% organic, with vegetarians and carnivores catered for and a menu that changes daily. As for Hamburg, it has more canals than Amsterdam, and its most scenic area is the Alster; cycle along waterfronts lined with cafés.

Price	€80–€115.
Rooms	23: 12 doubles, 5 singles, 3 suites, 3 apartments.
Meals	Dinner from €10. Wine from €13.
Closed	Never.
Directions	From Hamburg central station, metro U2 dir. Niendorf Nord stop Niendorf Markt; bus 191 dir. Grothwisch stop Burgwedeltwiete; hotel 100m. Or, from station, bus 5 dir. Burgwedel stop Burgwedelkamp; hotel 400m.

	Günter Dix
	Ökotel Hamburg,
	Holsteiner Chaussee 347,
	22457 Hamburg
Tel	+49 (0)40 559730 0
Email	info@oekotel.de
Web	www.oekotel.de

Ethical Collection: Environment; Food.
See page 211.

Price band: D

Kenner's Landlust

This was the first organic hotel in northern Germany, its green credentials matched only by its setting. The bright yellow half-timbered farmhouse on the forest edge was built in 1859 to shelter family, livestock and produce; now the friendly Kenners have created a green retreat for gregarious guests. You may not be waited on hand and foot, but there's plenty of freshly cooked, locally sourced organic food at mealtimes, and like-minded people to talk to… Kenny is the local authority on the wolves repopulating the area! Each light, comfortable bedroom has its own bathroom, and organic bed linen and towels. Downstairs, the oak-floored communal area is designed with a Scandinavian simplicity, sofas clustered around a cosy wood-burner. Wander into the kitchen whenever you want tea or coffee; visit the treatment room for shiatsu to sound therapy; there's a playroom for kids and free childcare in summer. As well as being 100% organically certified, the hotel draws its water from a nearby spring, and a cleansing system ensures only pristine water returns to the environment. It's seriously good value.

Price	€72–€80. Half board €53–€57 p.p. Full-board €61–€65 p.p.
Rooms	19: 10 doubles, 2 singles, 7 family rooms for 3-4.
Meals	Lunch buffet €10. Dinner buffet €17. Wine from €8.
Closed	Most of December.
Directions	From Hamburg, A7 south to Lüneburg; exit Dannenberg; 37km; at Göhrde, left for Dübbekold, 1.5km.

Ethical Collection: Food.
See page 211.

Price band: C

Familie Barbara & Kenny Kenner
Kenner's Landlust,
Dübbekold 1,
29473 Göhrde

Tel	+49 (0)58 559793 00
Email	info@kenners-landlust.de
Web	www.kenners-landlust.de

Biopension & Naturhotel Spöktal

Three generations of the Marold family have cared for this beautiful 20-hectare expanse of heathland, living in perfect tune with nature. Now four guest houses – dotted among the trees and heather – allow you too to experience what Eva-Maria calls the 'healing energy' of the place. For this dedicated family sustainability is not a set of guidelines, it's a way of life; 100% organic certification is just the tip of the iceberg. Water is piped from a spring in the garden, then solar heated. The four houses, all constructed in the last 40 years, are snugly insulated, with low-energy light bulbs fitted throughout. Local craftsmen use local materials, reclaimed wherever possible, and eco paints to decorate. Rooms are comfortable but simple – it's the great outdoors that's the attraction here. There's tons of space for kids to roam, and walks abound for more serious adventurers; a sauna under the stars is your reward. The delicious organic food is mostly vegetarian, but well-sourced meat and fish pop up on the menu, too. Happy guests have been coming here for 30-plus years.

Price	€82–€148. Half-board €60–€93 p.p.
Rooms	43 doubles, singles & suites.
Meals	Dinner, 2-4 courses, €8–€19. Wine from €9.
Closed	November; February.
Directions	From Hamburg, A7 for Hannover, exit Evendorf; thro' village, over main road & left to Steinbeck. Right at crossing, then left over river. After yellow sign, right. Spöktal signed.

Familie Marold
Biopension & Naturhotel Spöktal,
Haus Spöktal Marold OHG, Spöktal 1,
29646 Bispingen-Steinbeck

Tel	+49 (0)5194 2320
Email	info@spoektal.de
Web	www.spoektal.de

Ethical Collection: Environment; Food.
See page 211.

Price band: C

Entry 107   Map 4

Hotel Restaurant Flachshaus

Medieval cobbles, cascading window boxes, spruce houses and a church whose bells chime merrily from 7am. The sleepy town of Wachtendonk ('guard hill' in Dutch – Holland is close) is more picturesque than it sounds. The inn is divided into two halves: an elegant 18th-century townhouse with later extensions, and an older, quainter restaurant 50m away. Charming, hard-working Margarethe and husband Rolf have been running organic eateries since 1985 and have hospitality down to a fine art. The atmosphere is warmly inviting, the staff are lovely, the food is tasty, the bio wines are delicious and the feel is more restaurant-with-rooms than hotel. Indeed, there is more charm in the sweet old-fashioned restaurant – and the terraces – than in the rooms above, though they are perfectly comfortable, with their pastel print duvets on good firm beds. The better, bigger rooms are in the townhouse, with cheerful colours and wicker armchairs, white walls and fine old polished boards – and recycling bins on each landing. Breakfast is served at dining tables below, and there's a shop selling fairtrade goodies.

Price	€96–€114. Half-board €72–€81 p.p.
Rooms	9: 2 doubles, 1 family suite. Restaurant: 6 twins/doubles.
Meals	Lunch & dinner €24. Wine from €12.
Closed	Never.
Directions	From Venlo (in Holland), A40 dir. Duisburg. 5km from motorway. Or, train Düsseldorf-Kempen/Ndrh & bus 063 to Wachtendonk.

Ethical Collection: Food.
See page 211.

Price band: D

Herr Rolf Altena
Hotel Restaurant Flachshaus,
Weinstr. 5 & Feldstr. 29,
47669 Wachtendonk

Tel	+49 (0)2836 8494
Email	flachshaus@gmx.de
Web	www.hotel-flachshaus.de

Klosterhof Abtsberg

Little ones will love it here, on the edge of the Black Forest, surrounded by meadows, orchards and happy animals. This is a 'demonstration farm' that school children visit, a place where you can meet organically reared cows, horses, goats and sheep... and rabbits, cats and one bouncy guinea pig. Animal noises, animal smells, the hum of the tractor and the trilling of birds: this is farming at its most wholesome. The farm and the 1920s-built house were leased by the friendly young Hilschers in 1997; they have renovated, insulated and introduced eco showers and dual-flow loos. Boilers are fired with their own wood, old varieties of fruit tree are planted each year and the abundant spring water is their own. On the top floor is a simple apartment under the eaves with comfy beds, a mishmash of furniture and a decorative balcony with pastoral views. Outside are a sand box and swings, and – to purchase – home-produced beef, honey and wine. Arrive by train (free pick up), then hire bikes for your stay – Gengenbach's delightful and historic centre is a ten-minute ride. *Minimum stay two nights.*

Price	€270 per week.
Rooms	Apartment for 4.
Meals	Restaurant 2km.
Closed	Never.
Directions	Karlsrune-Basel A5 exit Oftenburg dir. Villingen-Schwenningen. Signs to Gengenbach; in town centre, right & follow railway; 2nd left after mini golf; 200m. Or, train to Gengenbach for free pick up.

Uli & Alexandra Hilscher
Klosterhof Abtsberg,
Abtsberg 4b,
77723 Gengenbach, Ortenaukreis
Tel   +49 (0)7803 980207
Email   suetterlin.hilscher@t-online.de
Web   www.klosterhof-abtsberg.de

Ethical Collection: Environment; Community; Food.
See page 211.

Price band: B

Scandinavia

Niilos Cabin

Get back to nature? This remote little cabin on a small green island is just the thing. Here, in Finland's south western archipelago, you are two hours from Helsinki yet fairytale forests with moss-covered floors, lakes for canoeing and beaches for swimming are outside the door. Experience frontier living in a house made from reclaimed materials. Organic market gardener Henrik and his green-fingered daughter Linnea have lived here for ten years, on the edge of a nature reserve crammed with moose and birdlife; they have also created an organic garden and arboretum from scratch, documented by Finnish TV. Linnea pops back from university at weekends to Henrik's new eco house 25m away – so the basic cabin with its bunk bed, ancient cooker and outhouse compost loo are yours. The market garden is brimful of fruit and vegetables if you want to whip up a (simple) meal; the arboretum contains almost every northern hemisphere tree in existence. Over dinner Henrik will inspire you with his knowledge of organic gardening, green construction and island life – he's something of a guru. *€5 discount for car-free travellers.*

Price	€50 per night.
Rooms	Cabin for 2 (bunk beds, kitchenette, shower & outhouse wc).
Meals	One dinner per visit included in price. Restaurant 1km.
Closed	Rarely.
Directions	From Ekenäs along Baggövägen 12km to south (ferry crossing half way). Right onto Skaldövägen, right to Sommarövagen. Guests can be picked up from Ekenäs.

Henrik & Linnea Nordström
Niilos Cabin,
Sommarövägen 76,
10600 Ekenäs, Nyland

Tel	+358 1920 1477
Email	henrik@seanet.com
Web	www.henriksgarden.com

Ethical Collection: Environment; Community; Food.
See page 211.

Price band: B

Labby-Kaarnaranta

Isnäs lies in that vast stretch of archipelago dotted with glassy deep-blue lakes and vibrantly coloured pine and birch forests, an hour east of Helsinki. Janne is a member of a young cooperative running a biodynamic, 40-hectare farm producing spelt wheat, herbs and vegetables; cattle, sheep and an indigenous horse graze. Labby-Kaarnaranta campaigns against nuclear energy and GM foods; several members belong to the Green Party, too. Knowledge is willingly shared, so courses from ecological building renovation to herbal medicine are on offer, alongside farm tours and nature trails. If you want to do your own thing, the lake is great for water sports, while on wet days you can head for the museums. The commune feeling extends to the lakeside B&B, housed in a converted sawmill office. It has a sociable kitchen with a huge table where you can tuck into organic dinners from the farm, and a community room warmed by a lovely Finnish stove. And you can stock up at the farm shop and do your own cooking. Bedrooms are simple and family-friendly, the best being the double with the lake view – spot the storks and cranes.

Price	€20-€30 p.p.
Rooms	5: 1 double, 1 single, 2 triples, 1 quadruple, all sharing bathrooms.
Meals	Breakfast €6. Dinner €12-€30. BYO. Guest kitchen.
Closed	Rarely.
Directions	From Porvoo follow 1571 for 22km, signed Isnäs. From T-junc. in Isnäs, signs to Kaarnaranta.

Ethical Collection: Food.
See page 211.

Price band: B

Mr Janne Länsipuro
Labby-Kaarnaranta,
Edöntie 142,
07750 Isnäs, Eastern Uusimaa

Mobile	+358 4075 33524
Email	info@juurakko.fi
Web	www.juurakko.fi

Ongajok Mountain Farm

It may be a long and bumpy road to get here, but the rushing waters of the many rivers you pass will have you lacing up your walking boots the moment you arrive. The commitment to nature and the environment is as genuine here as the welcome. Softly-spoken Espen is a chef by training, and has converted this remote traditional Norwegian farmhouse into a flourishing centre for outdoor activities where the delicious food is as reviving as the fresh arctic air. The cuisine is Sami with a gourmet touch – reindeer, grouse, halibut, cod, forest berries, even boar and seal – and the cakes and breads are homemade. Mountains dominate the landscape while silence permeates the ambience. The pine-lined rooms with their Nordic Swan certified towels and smellies are very basic (and include en suite compost toilets), but you can lounge around in the main building's cosy log-fired sitting room. And if you feel like braving the night air, there's a hot tub in which to soothe your aching muscles as you gaze on the galaxy in all its glory. Green energy consumes this special place. Great for groups.

Price	Half-board 1,790 NOK-2,090 NOK p.p. Minimum 6 people.
Rooms	16 rooms for 1-2.
Meals	Half-board only.
Closed	Never.
Directions	Directions on booking.

Espen Ottem
Ongajok Mountain Farm,
Mathisdalen,
9518 Alta, Finnmark

Tel	+47 7843 2600
Email	espen@ongajok.no
Web	www.ongajok.no

Ethical Collection: Environment; Food.
See page 211.

Price band: G

Engholm Husky Lodge

Arrive to the call of 50 working huskies, their ghostly howls from the compound rushing through the pines to the porch of your turf-sprouting hut. Naturally snug and seated around suspended stone tables beneath moose-antler lights, guests pluck wine glasses from their clever rigging and consider when to slip into alcove beds. Kitchenettes are at your disposal, but full-board means eating fresh salmon and moose meat in the 'Barta', a communal hut where everyone sits on reindeer skins around the fire – following a hot tub or sauna. Two cabins have private bathrooms and running water, but it's not a hardship to fill up your water bucket or share the bathroom and compost loos, especially when they, like everything, have been built by Sven himself, a master craftsman whose hand-made utopia this is. Go slow is his policy (why not canoe to the Sami Parliament instead of drive?) – except when he's winning the trans-Arctic sled race (for the 11th time). Which makes him, along with Viking-haired Christel, one of the best instructors in the art of dog 'mushing' across the frozen tundra, under the Northern Lights.

Price	From 700 NOK.
Rooms	8 cabins: 3 for 3, 2 for 4, 1 for 8, 2 for 9. Most share bathrooms.
Meals	Breakfast 100 NOK. Dinner 250 NOK. Wine 260 NOK. Guest kitchenettes.
Closed	Never.
Directions	From Karasjok, west for 6km. Road 72 direction Kotokeino. Signed.

Ethical Collection: Environment; Food.
See page 211.

Price band: C

Sven Engholm
Engholm Husky Lodge,
9730 Karasjok, Finnmark

Tel   +47 9158 6625
Email   post@engholm.no
Web   www.engholm.no

Fogdegården Borten

Merete is an extraordinary woman, bringing up two young children by herself, and rearing lambs, pigs, Shetland ponies… and a recalcitrant cow and her calf, too. Her conservative Norwegian neighbours aren't sure how to handle this whirlwind of a lady, who in previous incarnations has been a vet, a civil engineer and a member of the national underwater rugby team. Now this low-intensity organic farm is her passion and she looks set to stay, much to the delight of one smart Trondheim restaurant which she supplies with vegetables. Her cherries and eggs also come highly recommended, but it's the potatoes that seal the victory and customers at her daily market stall are prepared to pay premium prices. You'll get to try them, too, as you sit down to supper in the farmhouse kitchen, more often than not alongside volunteer workers. A stay here is a communal experience, best enjoyed if you muck in: milking, feeding, picking, harvesting the hay…as much or as little as you like. Upstairs, the rooms reflect the prevailing ethic: not luxurious but simple and good, and there's one bathroom for everyone.

Price	1,320 NOK.
Rooms	2: 1 double, 1 twin sharing bath.
Meals	Dinner 100 NOK-275 NOK. By arrangement. BYO.
Closed	October-April.
Directions	From Trondheim, E6 south to Ler. Left onto RV704; left at sign to Kirkfla, then right at 2nd sign to Kirkfla; farm 200m on right. Or, train to Storen, Heimdal or Trondheim; bus stops outside farm.

Merete Støving
Fogdegården Borten,
Ler, 7234 Nr. Trondheim,
Sør-Trøndelag

Tel	+47 7285 0556
Email	mestovr@hotmail.com
Web	www.fogdegarden.com

Ethical Collection: Community; Food.
See page 211.

Price band: D

Entry 114   Map 4

Amble Gaard

There are many ways of getting here. One is through one of the longest road-tunnels in Europe; the other, a tremendous ferry journey through the longest fjord in Norway (the Sognefjord), whose convergent hillsides tenderly pinch at Kaupanger to shape the loveliest of harbours. A spectator to this, up on the hillside close to where the venison is hung to dry, is a thunder box pagoda worthy of Thor himself, inscribed with a poem on proper etiquette; one of the more unusual legacies of the Heiberg family, who have been farming, foresting, haymaking and hunting on this land since 1690. Ingebjörg and Gjert are the current incumbents, both generous and helpful: she looks after the guests, he the organic farm. All five of the handsomely timbered self-catering guesthouses are built from, and heated by, wood harvested on site; and they're spaced for privacy in spruce clearings above the orchards and main house. Each has its distinctive colour and history; there's an organic café for snacks and also a campsite on the bay, supplied with free firewood and running water. Sail and swim in the fjord or head for walks in the forest and mountain.

Price	4,000 NOK–16,800 NOK per week. Camping 40 NOK per tent per night.
Rooms	5 houses sleeping 4-12. Campsite for 30 tents.
Meals	Restaurant 4km.
Closed	November–March.
Directions	From Oslo, E16 to Lærdal, Road 5 Sogndal-Fodnes; car ferry to Manhiller; 7km to Kaupanger dir. Timberlid & Øvre Amla. Signed from white house. Or, train to Fläm, bus to Gudvangen, ferry to Kaupanger. Owners will meet on arrival.

Ethical Collection: Environment.
See page 211.

Price band: C

Ingebjörg & Gjert Strand Heiberg
Amble Gaard,
6854 Kaupanger,
Sogn og Fjordane

Tel	+47 5767 8170
Email	post@amblegaard.no
Web	www.amblegaard.no

Fretheim Hotel

Sitting white and trimly timbered, its sheer glass atrium resplendent, Fretheim surveys the harbour community of Flåm much like the cruise ships that cut their way through a spectacular World Heritage filigree of fjords. But while the ferries and trans-alpine trains come and go, this hotel-cum-farm has been at the centre of things since 1870. Swedish owner, Birgittha, is keen to champion the locality and has dedicated a whole section of the Per Sivle library (a local poet rescued from obscurity) to disappearing Nynorsk literature. But she has brought a modern sophistication too and the 121 bedrooms display an earthy cool kind of chic. However, the 'conscience kitchen' is her signature mark and she puts her money where her mouth is, paying above the odds to local farmers and the agricultural college for organic lamb, fruit and veg. Cured meats are smoked out back, close to a regimented recycling system, then hung in traditional storehouses above a hearty feasting table. Guests are invited to lend all hands to the horse and plough for the planting of the new season's potatoes; savour slow food at its very best.

Price	1,090 NOK–1,700 NOK.
Rooms	121 doubles, triples & quadruples.
Meals	Summer buffet 395 NOK. Winter à la carte menu. Wine from 295 NOK.
Closed	Christmas to end January.
Directions	From Bergen/Oslo, E16 to Flåm. Or, by train from Oslo/Bergen to Flåm, change at Myrdal or express boat Bergen-Flåm.

	Birgittha Sandstöm & Jan Fredrik Hagen
	Fretheim Hotel,
	Pb 63, 5742 Flåm, Sogn og Fjordane
Tel	+47 5763 6300
Email	mail@fretheim-hotel.no
Web	www.fretheim-hotel.no

Ethical Collection: Food.
See page 211.

Price band: E

Ullershov Gård

Per had to learn fast the art of low-intensity, organic dairy farming, but he put his architect skills to good use, and converted the 16th-century storage barn, high on its stilts, into a two-bed guest house. Now its cosy rooms and four-posters are covered in the softest handmade quilts, and all is warmed by a furnace fed on biomass waste from the forest. The yew-tree garden is a popular choice for weddings while the herb garden, seemingly wild, is the result of careful husbandry, producing infinite varieties of mint – which celebrated chef (and Per's wife) Ingar-Marie uses to mouthwatering effect in her stuffed trout. Dine in the main house – where there are two further bedrooms – seated on carved chairs with a Viking dragon motif; or breakfast in the pantry at the long wooden table, selecting cheesy and fishy delicacies from a tantalising carousel, the air redolent of bread-making. Then repair to the sitting room for an erudite read; or upstairs to Ingar-Marie's textile museum – an astonishing collection of antique outfits and poignant stories of the women who wore them. *Farmhouse for five also available.*

Price	800 NOK.
Rooms	4: 2 doubles; 2 twins/doubles in main house sharing bath.
Meals	Breakfast 75 NOK. Lunch 75 NOK. Dinner 100 NOK. Restaurants 5km.
Closed	Never.
Directions	From Kløfta, E6 to Vormsund, or bus from central station to Nes Kirke, or train to Lillestrøm, change for Årnes. Owners can arrange collection.

Ethical Collection: Environment; Food.
See page 211.

Price band: C

	Per & Ingar-Marie Ødegaard
	Ullershov Gård,
	2160 Vormsund,
	2160 Østlandet, Akershus
Tel	+47 6390 2740
Email	ullerhov@online.no
Web	www.ullershov.no

Aurora Retreat

"Blissful", you'll sigh, resting the oars and drifting down-river, toward where you'll be smoking a brace of freshly caught perch. "Purging", you'll breathe in the sauna as your nostrils gently steam; shouting "bracing" as you cool off in the snow under the shimmering Aurora. Purity accompanies a stay here, partly to do with the old vicarage that has been sensitively converted and reclaimed into the guest house. The finish is truly restorative, whether in the shared breakfast or sitting rooms, or upstairs meditating in the tiny alcove attached to one of the bedrooms – even in the composting toilet that asks gentlemen for environmentally careful aim. But most nourishing are the company of Mikael and Maya who live with their two daughters in an outbuilding full of creativity and the smell of freshly baked bread from the wood-oven. Their belief in holistic well-being explains much: why they have no car (they will hire one to pick up guests), why they recycle all their water and conserve their energy, and why their wholesome vegetarian food – unique in Lapland – is so high in nutrients and life-energy.

Price	790 SEK.
Rooms	6: 3 doubles en suite; 3 twins sharing bath.
Meals	Breakfast 80 SEK. Lunch 125 SEK. Dinner 150 SEK. Wine from 200 SEK.
Closed	Never.
Directions	From Kiruna, E10 dir. Svappavaara; E45 dir. Vittangi; route 395 dir. Junosuando. Or, train to Kiruna & Gallivare. Owner can arrange pick up.

Maya Rao & Mikael Kangar
Aurora Retreat,
Folketshusvagen 37, PO Box 196,
98062 Junosuando, Pajala

Tel	+46 (0)978 30061
Email	info@auroraretreat.se
Web	www.auroraretreat.se

Ethical Collection: Environment; Food.
See page 211.

Price band: C

Vindelåforsens Stugby

Travel by public transport to this Sami land of vast alpine heaths and lakes, quick rivers and lush birch forests and 20% gets taken off your bill. As a central figure in Ammarnäs, Urban has inherited his father's sense of purpose that saw the rescue of a bunch of prefab components in the 80s, the assembly of the self-catering houses and apartments, and the carving of a tractor/snow-mobile road to Lake Bertejaure, where you'll find the very simple fishing cabins. Functionality is forgiven by sound eco principles, which have determined important choices: 'eco-fibre' insulation (recycled newspapers), hydroelectric mains supply, warmth from 'thermo-grounding' (heat absorption) and wood you've cut yourself... and the sewage separation system, which provides both natural compost and fertiliser. There is real heart here as well. Marita is a talented sculptress, producing work that captures all the vitality and compassion of life; she even cast the king's head for the 10 krona coin. She uses her intuition when giving massage too, channelling the body's healing energy to wherever, as she puts it, "is making faces".

Price	Houses €430–€540. Apartments €430. Huts €225–€320. Prices per week.
Rooms	5 houses for 8. 2 apartments for 5. 8 huts for 2-3.
Meals	Restaurant 2km.
Closed	Never.
Directions	E45 from Östersund to Sorsele, or road 363 from Umeå. From Ammarnäs village, 2km: follow signs to 'Norra Ammarnäs'. Or, bus to Ammarnäs, owners pick up.

Ethical Collection: Environment.
See page 211.

Price band: A

Urban Berglund & Marita Norin
Vindelåforsens Stugby,
92075 Ammarnäs, Sorsele

Tel	+46 (0)952 61100
Email	urban@bertejaure.se
Web	www.bertejaure.se

Dala-Floda Inn

Draped in bucolic abundance and cushioned by a pretty herb garden, the inn looks fresh
from holiday-in-Provence with gifts for everyone, not least the birds who love the berries.
Everyone else heads toward the weathered 'restaurant' sign, for the very best of Slow Food
country cooking, important to welcoming new owner, Evalotta. Consider that 70% of the
food here is from local organic farms, as you savour the lamb and meet the return guests,
who decide over a mouthful of Swedish caviar pancake that the inn is a highlight of the
beautiful Dalarna river region; even the compost is treated to a rich diet. After dinner,
choose an animal ring to save your napkin for breakfast, before making your way back to
the guest house, where downstairs you'll find a library well stocked with foreign literature
and two exhibition studios, one brooding with heavy 'mood' pieces, the other reflecting
sunnier dispositions. Throughout are objets d'art collected on the former owners' travels
in India and Africa; but the rooms are traditional and good, you rest on sweet iron
bedsteads and look out onto the lake.

Price	£89-£125 (sterling). Half-board £175 for 2.
Rooms	17: 8 doubles, 7 singles, 2 family rooms.
Meals	Dinner, four courses, £16-£32. Wine from £18.
Closed	Christmas.
Directions	Directions on booking. Or, train from Stockholm to Dala-Floda village, change at Borlänge; inn 3km from village, owners will collect.

Evalotta & Per Ersson
Dala-Floda Inn,
Badvägen 6,
78044 Dala-Floda

Tel   +46 (0)241 22050
Email   info@dalafloda-vardshus.se
Web   www.dalafloda-vardshus.se

Ethical Collection: Food.
See page 211.

Price band: D

Kolarbyn Eco-Lodge

Come with an acceptance of simplicity and you'll love it here, deep in the forest. Wise delegation is recommended: a couple of beefy hands for the chopping and splicing of wood, a light pair for the gathering of old newspapers from the recycling shed, and a careful pair for cooking over the camp fire with the most rudimentary of utensils and a kettle as black as any pot. The turf-covered hobbit dens, large enough for a plain sheepskin-covered single bed on either side and a wood-burning stove at the end, are the craziest, snuggest sleeping quarters in Sweden – probably the greenest too, built from 'garbage planks' from the local saw mill; there's no electricity on site either, so have those candles lit before dark. Nor any running water, so it's the lake for washing, the creek for the dishes, and the composting toilet-throne for serious thought. The forest quickly becomes a second home: that's what Marcus thinks, the young and hugely enthusiastic entrepreneur who started it all and now runs night-time moose and wolf safaris. His next project is a floating sauna on the lake – madly brilliant.

Ethical Collection: Environment; Community; Food.
See page 211.

Price band: B

Price	500 SEK.
Rooms	12 huts for 2. Child bed available.
Meals	Restaurant 3km.
Closed	Rarely.
Directions	From Stockhom, E18 to Västeras; routes 66 & 233 to Skinnskatteberg; Kolarbyn 3km before village. Or, by train from Stockholm to Köping, then bus 500 to Skinnskatteberg.

Marcus Jonson
Kolarbyn Eco-Lodge,
orntorpets, 73992 Kursgard,
Skinnskatteberg
Tel +46 (0)704 007053
Email info@kolarbyn.se
Web kolarbyn.se

Charlottendals Gård

Järna is home to Swedish anthroposophy (spirituality meets biodynamic agriculture) and to Peter, a former eco journalist who has created among a small community of families a working model for the Transitional way of life. Get the basics right: here, waste disposal literally sorts the solids from the non-solids, to be transformed into crop spray or by worms into the secret compost behind the tumbling vegetable garden. Yet eco-crusty this is not. Electricity is either solar or wind generated, Peter's car runs on natural gas diesel, while the new main house, made of clay, dung and timber, designed with light in mind and eco fibre insulation at its heart, divides to form a quirky, minimal and open-plan mezzanine apartment to one side. Down the spiral staircase is Peter's in-house cinema, where you can see his documentary on the impact of giant dam building in India. His joyful wife, Merle, sings Estonian folk songs to her children on the accordion and runs the kindergarten, which occupies the lower half of a separate building – below the second (and very private) apartment, which is perfect for young families.

Price	4,500 SEK per week. Linen 150 SEK p.p.
Rooms	2 apartments: 1 for 2, 1 for 5.
Meals	Restaurant and shop 7km.
Closed	Never.
Directions	From Stockholm, E4 to Järna or train from Stockholm to Södertälje Syd, change at Järna. Owner will arrange collection.

	Peter & Merle Hagerrot
	Charlottendals Gård,
	7 Järna, 15395 Södertälje
Tel	+46 (0)855 170097
Email	peter.hagerrot@telia.com
Web	www.charlottendal.se

Ethical Collection: Environment; Community. See page 211.

Price band: C

Tisenö Gård

For generations, the family island that floats gracefully on Lake Tisnaren has been synonymous with inventiveness. The 'ferry' that fetches you from the mainland is a wonderful makeshift enterprise, powered by an old tractor engine and crewed by Gilly, the needy sausage dog. Then there are the crayfish cages that son Eric uses, designed by his grandfather, the natural sewage system that channels water from the lake, and the clay house (for courses), hand-built with mud, straw and dung. Just as each member of the family (they live across the paddock) gets on with their jobs on this 125-hectare organic cattle farm, you self-cater in the lovely, mellowing yellow farmhouse, with its simple rustic rooms and warmest of kitchen tables. Be sure to bring your own supplies (no shops for miles), but you can graze from the veggie gardens and pick the delicious wild mushrooms. For complete privacy, you can even stay in a cabin on your own tiny atoll. But do spend time with Isabella, who keeps things uncommercial and whose bright humour and love of dance leaves one feeling rejuvenated.

Price	House 7,500 SEK. Lake cabin 2,500 SEK. Prices per week.
Rooms	House for 8-10. Lake cabin for 4 (bunk beds).
Meals	Restaurant 15km.
Closed	Call in advance.
Directions	Directions by car on booking. Or, train to Katrineholm; owners will arrange collection.

Ethical Collection: Environment; Food.
See page 211.

Price band: A

Isabella Hermelin
Tisenö Gård,
61014 Lake Tisnaren,
Östergötland

Tel   +46 (0)151 22054
Email   isabella.hermelin@swipnet.se
Web   www.tiseno.se

Handelsman Flink

Evert Taube, Sweden's famous troubadour, came to the island to deal with 'personal problems' and ended up writing a ballad inspired by the sight of a local lass rowing to shore. Now a rock is dedicated to him and everyone joins in the singing on musical evenings. Stefan, a life-long hotelier, saw potential here years ago when it was just the original shop; now, as it was in 1912, it's the perfect place for anyone hankering after Swedish sweets and nostalgia. Wonderful, too, to see the hotel fisherman carry a bristling catch of crayfish straight from his boat into the kitchen; and to taste organic meat and cheese from local farms, garnished with herbs from the flowerbeds and washed down with Bohuslän beer: all reasons why this restaurant was awarded the prestigious SWAN mark for organic excellence. Then it's an easy stumble back to this island intimacy of 12 rooms, all sea-light and breezy under terracotta – honeymooners to the detached, mezzanine 'Sea Suite' right on the water, and families to the 'Heaven Suite' with its terrace panorama of the calmingly distant mainland.

Price	SEK 1,780-SEK 3,200.
Rooms	12: 10 doubles, 1 suite, 1 family room.
Meals	Dinner, 3 courses, SEK 425. À la carte also menu available. Wine from SEK 285.
Closed	Never.
Directions	From Göteburg, E6 dir. Tjörn & Orust, Varekil-Ellös; take ferry from Fröjdendal. Or, train to Stenungsund, bus to Henån, bus to Kärehogen, & ferry.

Stefan Hjelmér
Handelsman Flink,
Flatön, 47491 Ellös, Orust
Tel   +46 (0)304 55051
Email   info@handelsmanflink.se
Web   www.handelsmanflink.se

Ethical Collection: Food.
See page 211.

Price band: G

Entry 124   Map 4

Carlton Hotel Guldsmeden

Copenhagen's first Guldsmeden hotel – in a tall townhouse above a supermarket in creative Vesterbro. Reception is a café with a hip-hostel air where guests gather to swap tales; breakfast is wholesome and help-yourself – to vanilla yoghurt with honey and almonds, or brown-bread muesli with blueberries. Some bedrooms lie in the interesting, quirky, timber-framed outhouse, reached by steep stairs (or lift); others are in the main house; all have a slightly different feel from the rooms in the sister hotels. There's dark wood furniture from a Balinese community project and fun armchairs upholstered in cow hide, rich patterned bedspreads, soft lighting and an organic mini-bar. Scrumptious sandwiches will keep you going as you explore wonderful Copenhagen; visit Christiania, Denmark's 'free city' (no street lights, no cars) set up by 1970s eco pioneers, and the famous Tivoli Gardens, best enjoyed at night. Or simply stroll the streets and gaze on the exquisite architecture. When you leave, give something back: all Guldsmeden guests are asked to donate to the Children's Heart Foundation.

Price	1,045 DKK-1,595 DKK.
	Suites 1,640 DKK-2,495 DKK.
Rooms	64 doubles, singles & suites.
Meals	Restaurants nearby.
Closed	Christmas (open New Year).
Directions	Directions on booking.

Ethical Collection: Community; Food.
See page 211.

Price band: E

Sandra & Marc Weinert
Carlton Hotel Guldsmeden,
Vesterbrogade 66, København V,
DK-1620 Copenhagen

Tel	+45 3322 1500
Email	booking@hotelguldsmeden.com
Web	www.hotelguldsmeden.dk/carlton/

Bertrams Hotel Guldsmeden

The Hotel Guldsmeden clan have a unique approach to organic-chic, yet each of their hotels is different. Sitting above an organic deli, Bertrams' country kitchen has exposed beams and windows that allow you to watch the action. Here, people-watchers linger over a buffet-style breakfast, and the friendly and energetic staff 'hang out', always on hand for advice or a chat; equally sociable is the oasis garden. Wooden floors and sweet bamboo four-posters (from a Balinese community project) create a simple, tropical feel, yet the rooms are cosy and luxurious: feather duvets, thick cotton sheets, Persian rugs, kimonos, and wet rooms with stone sinks (but no shower curtains!). Choose between a view onto the bustling streets or the pretty cobbled courtyard, where barbecues are held in summer. Retro clothes shops and bohemian bars characterise Vesterbro – the red light district of old – while the quayside restaurants and elegant old boats of Nyhavn are a short cycle ride away. Bikes are on free loan. Superb. *Supporters of the Children's Heart Foundation.*

Price	1,180 DKK–1,795 DKK. Suites 1,640 DKK–2,995 DKK.
Rooms	47 doubles, singles & suites.
Meals	225 DKK. Wine (by the glass) from 45 DKK.
Closed	Christmas (open New Year)
Directions	Directions on booking.

	Sandra & Marc Weinert
	Bertrams Hotel Guldsmeden,
	Vesterbrogade 107, København V,
	DK-1620 Copenhagen
Tel	+45 3325 0405
Email	bertrams@hotelguldsmeden.com
Web	www.hotelguldsmeden.dk/bertrams/

Ethical Collection: Community; Food. See page 211.

Price band: F

Entry 126   Map 4

Axel Hotel Guldsmeden

A cobble's throw from the central station, Hotel Axel, the newest and largest of the Guldsmeden 'organic-chic' group, is a peaceful, soothing retreat. Step into the exotic baths of the spa, sink into reception's soft sofas, escape to the oasis garden at the back. Hotel Axel is all about being soothed, organically, so everything from the food on the oh-so-stylish tables to the bathroom treats in refillable containers is chemical free... even the spa and beauty products come straight from the hotel's (open-to-view) kitchen. And what better way of relieving the limbs after a day spent touring the cobbled streets of Copenhagen than an ayurvedic massage or a candlelit steam bath? Replenishing the soul doesn't stop here; you can also sample the organic delights of the quirky restaurant and the speciality cocktails. As for the bedrooms, they have a boutique-natural feel, with original art on the walls and furniture hand-crafted in Bali. Most have balconies with street views, but for the ultimate indulgence, go for the penthouse suite and the rooftop hot tub.
Supporters of the Children's Heart Foundation.

Price	1,145 DKK–1,995 DKK. Suites 2,195 DKK–4,995 DKK.
Rooms	129: 128 doubles, twins, singles & suites; 1 bunk room for 2.
Meals	Lunch & dinner 250 DKK. Wine from 150 DKK.
Closed	Never.
Directions	Directions on booking.

Ethical Collection: Community; Food.
See page 211.

Price band: F

Sandra & Marc Weinert
Axel Hotel Guldsmeden,
Helgolandsgade 7-11, København V,
DK-1653 Copenhagen

Tel	+45 3331 3266
Email	axel@hotelguldsmeden.com
Web	www.hotelguldsmeden.dk/axel/

Hotel Hellnar

The first business in Iceland to be certified for sustainable management is a haven of warmth and well-being wedged between the wave-lashed harbour and a wall of black basalt lava, at the foot of the brooding, ice-clad volcano Snæfellsjökull. Originally conceived as a spiritual retreat by kind-hearted owner Gudrun, the lodge is single-storey and built with eco-architectural principles: the sun stays indoors during the summer, small windows keep the cold out in winter, simplicity reigns. Shades of blue, yellow and white mirror the surrounding natural features of sea, light and ice. Bright and modern, each of the rooms has a compact shower and uninterrupted sea or glacier views. In the dining room expect the freshest of home-cooking and wide ocean views: lamb reared in the wilderness; fish from the rich glacial source; Icelandic bilberry pancakes (exquisite). Multiple languages will be spoken! Stay up for the midnight sun as it illuminates the crater summit… sooner or later the lure of a fluffy duvet and soft cotton sheets will have you horizontal, lulled to sleep by the plaintive wail of restless kittiwakes.

Price	€125–€155. Singles €110–€135. Extra child's bed €45–€52.
Rooms	20 twins. Extra child beds.
Meals	Lunch & dinner available.
Closed	October–April.
Directions	From Reykjavik, Rd 1 to Borgarnes; 2nd exit at r'bout onto Rd 54; to junction with Rd 574 (approx. 1 hr); left & drive for 19km, left to Hellnar; 1st left & drive past church.

Gudrun Bergmann
Hotel Hellnar,
Brekkubær Hellnar,
356 Snæfekksbær

Tel	+354 (0)435 6820
Email	hotel@hellnar.is
Web	www.hellnar.is

Ethical Collection: Environment. See page 211.

Price band: D

Southern Europe

Pálacio Belmonte

National Heritage status forbids solar panels, but that's not stopped French owner Frédéric Coustols from making this EU-subsidised restoration as 'green' as can be; his book on using lime in restoration has changed Portuguese law. More intimate house than hotel, this exquisite 600-year-old palace lives down a cobbled passage on the summit of one of Lisbon's hills. Each understated but ravishingly decorated suite is as big as a house and has a balcony or terrace with superlative views. The Bartolomeu de Gusmão dominates one of the Moorish towers, its octagonal sitting room, bedroom and bathroom on three levels, linked by a spiral stone stair; the Padre Himalaya is bliss in its Roman tower, with circular views of the city. Be seduced by wild silks in warm colours, heated terracotta tiles underfoot, quirky antiques and baskets of herbs, fruits and spices. Bathrooms (some small) are in white marble, lime mortar gives the original masonry a soft patina and corridors are polished stone: luxury at its simple best. The pool is heavenly – black marble with wooden decking, fringed by orange and lemon trees.

Price	€375–€2,500.
Rooms	11 suites.
Meals	Catering for groups & special requests only. Restaurants close by.
Closed	Rarely.
Directions	Directions on booking.

Marta Mendonça
Pálacio Belmonte,
Páteo Dom Fradique 14,
1100-624 Lisbon, Estremadura

Tel	+351 218 816600
Email	office@palaciobelmonte.com
Web	www.palaciobelmonte.com

Ethical Collection: Environment.
See page 211.

Price band: G

Quinta do Rio Touro

The Reino family have planted over 5,000 trees on their farm in the Sintra-Cascais Natural Park. Lush organic gardens heave with fruit – peaches, bananas, grapefruit, oranges, apples, plums, strawberries and, above all, limes. Feel free to pick your own. Green waste is collected for tasty tree mulch and Senhor Reino is something of an expert on ecology and the organic movement (scour his library – 7,000 books, mostly on the subject). Scented jasmine tumbles over the entrance to the solar-heated manor house, along with an eclectic collection of artefacts: Roman pots, Moroccan stone-carved tables, antique fans. Your hosts worked in the diplomatic field for many years and are well-travelled; Senhor Reino will like nothing more than to help you plan your own journey. Choose a traditional Portuguese room with a balcony and a sea view or go for a touch more privacy in the little house at the foot of the garden. The locally sourced organic breakfasts are outstanding: home-laid eggs, local pastries, fresh cheeses, pumpkin chutney, and their own honey. *Saltwater pool.*

Price	€120-€200. Singles from €110.
Rooms	8: 4 doubles, 2 suites for 2-4. Garden house: 2 suites.
Meals	Restaurant 500m.
Closed	Rarely.
Directions	A5 towards Cascais, junc.12 for Malveira; right for 8km; left at signs for Azoia/Cabo da Roca, left again. Signed, past 1st house.

Ethical Collection: Environment; Food.
See page 211.

Price band: E

Fernando & Maria Gabriela Reino
Quinta do Rio Touro,
Caminho do Rio Touro, Azoia, Cabo da
Roca, 2705-001 Sintra, Estremadura

Tel	+351 219 292862
Email	info@quinta-riotouro.com
Web	www.quinta-riotouro.com

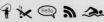

Cerro da Fontinha

Miguel has used natural, locally sourced materials in these inspiring self-catering cottages. The simple character of simple dwellings has been preserved, and funky, chunky touches added. And to reveal the fabric of the building Miguel has left visible areas of *taipa* so you can see the mix of soil and stones between lath and plaster. Everything is as natural as can be: showers have stone bases and terracotta surrounds, a bunk bed has a carved ladder and fat wooden legs. Pebbles embedded in walls create coat and towel hooks, thick cuts of wood become mantelpieces, stone sofas are cosily cushioned. There are alcoves for oil and vinegar, curving work surfaces and cheerful stripes and gingham. Rainwater is harvested for your shower, reed beds collect waste. You have countryside on the doorstep, a eucalyptus wood for shade, good restaurants and Carvalhal beach nearby – hire mountain bikes to get there. There's also a little lake for swimming, and fishing and ceramic workshops for children who wish to learn a local skill. Ask for a delicious organic veg box.

Price	€110–€170 for 2 nights (€385–€595 per week).
Rooms	6 cottages; 2 for 2, 4 for 4.
Meals	Restaurants nearby.
Closed	Rarely.
Directions	From Faro A22 to Lagos, N120 though Aljezur for São Teotónio. 5km after crossing into Alentejo, left to Brejão, 1st left. House on right after lake. Or, train from Faro to Lagos, then bus to Odeceixe.

Senhor Miguel Godinho
Cerro da Fontinha,
Turismo da Natuereza Lda, Brejão,
7630-575 São Teótonio, Alentejo

Tel	+351 282 949083
Email	info@cerrodafontinha.com
Web	www.cerrodafontinha.com

Ethical Collection: Environment; Community.
See page 211.

Price band: C

Monte da Bravura

Organic orange trees! Fifty of them, laden with sun-drenched fruits waiting to wake you up, freshly squeezed. Hens! Free-range, organic-fed, for your morning eggs. Figs, grapes, plums and pears, flourishing, chemical free, in the garden – beneficial for the biodiversity of the region... and the breakfast jams. Elisabete and Fernando, who built this complex from scratch years ago, are proud of their work to protect the flora and fauna of the gorgeous Barragem, and justly so: the lagoon they founded is a safe house to local species, birds and bees who spread a pure seed. Curious minds are encouraged; the inquisitive may stumble across a lesson in centuries-old, non-intensive crop farming in the museum. Indoors, an imaginative use of antiques on display: tables from old carts, an old trough for the cutlery, wall partitions from excavated local stone. Given the collection, the bedrooms and apartments are surprisingly uncluttered; heavy curtains keep rooms dark, but flick open to let in the distant glow of night-time lights over Lagos. Security and alarm systems abound. Tempting menus are garden-fresh. Organic. Botanic.

Price	€95–€140.
Rooms	12 suites for 2-4 (5 with kitchenettes).
Meals	Lunch & dinner with wine €20–€30, by arrangement. Restaurants 0.5km.
Closed	November–February.
Directions	From Lagos to Vila de Odiaxere; follow signs to Barragem de Bravura; pass windmill on right, on for approx. 5km, gate on left.

Ethical Collection: Environment; Food.
See page 211.

Price band: D

Elisabete & Fernando Madeira
Monte da Bravura,
Cotifo, Caixa Postal 1003 F,
8600-077 Lagos, Algarve

Tel	+351 282 688175
Email	info@montedabravura.com
Web	www.montedabravura.com

Casa Grande da Fervenza

The river Miño is a stone's throw from this house and ancient working mill. The 18 hectares of ancient woodland that girdle it won the 2007 Forest of the Year prize and it has been declared a Unesco Biosphere Reserve. The Casa, named after the amazing rocky waterfall outside, is both hotel-restaurant and working museum; delightful staff will give you a guided tour. There's a cosy bar, and the restaurant, with its own spring, glorious open fireplace and wood-fired oven, is in the oldest part, dating from the 17th century. Locally sourced menus are based on traditional regional specialities – suckling pig, wild boar stew – and wines are the region's best. After a day out walking or on the river (with canoe or traditional *batuxo*) return to quiet and simple bedrooms; it's worth paying for one of the larger ones. The restoration has been meticulous in its respect for local tradition: country furniture has been restored, rugs woven on their own looms, there are linen curtains, chestnut beams and hand-painted sinks. There's no stinting on creature comforts here but the setting is the thing.

Price	€61–€76. Singles €49–€61. Suite €80–€100.
Rooms	9: 8 doubles, 1 suite.
Meals	Breakfast €8. Lunch & dinner €20. À la carte €20–€30.
Closed	Never.
Directions	From Madrid/La Coruña A-6 exit km488 marker. N-VI for Lugo. 2km to Conturiz & left at r'bout by Hotel Torre de Núñez for Páramo; 11km; right at A Fervenza sign; 1km.

Norman Pérez Sánchez-Orozco
Casa Grande da Fervenza,
Ctra. Lugo-Páramo km11,
27163 O Corgo, Lugo

Tel	+34 982 150610
Email	info@fervenza.com
Web	www.fervenza.com

Ethical Collection: Environment; Community.
See page 211.

Price band: C

Entry 133   Map 5

Posada Molino del Canto

Lying in a primeval Eden-like valley, lapped by the river Ebro, this stunning 13th-century millworkers' home has been restored using local, reclaimed and eco-friendly materials by young owner Javier. From the dim little entrance hall you enter a chunky-beamed, stone-walled sitting room scattered with country furniture, a sofa, and a stove crackling with sustainable wood. Then to bedrooms upstairs, each a splendid surprise: a cosy, delightful sitting area downstairs with a sofabed for children, and a double on the mezzanine (hot in summer?). There are antique wrought-iron beds, large classic wardrobes, white-and-terracotta bathrooms (grey water is filtered and recycled), sky windows to gaze at the stars... and you drift off to the sound of the river. Breakfast is a fine start to the day and the fresh seasonal dinners (veg from their organic patch) are memorable. On a promontory down by the river is the watermill, 1,000 years old; the old flint wheels spin into action still when the sluice gate is opened. Look out for interesting birds; Javier is helping to compile a census for the Ornithological Society.

Price	€83. Singles €71. Plus VAT at 7%.
Rooms	6: 3 doubles, 3 twins. Extra beds available.
Meals	Tapas-style lunch €5–€10. Dinner, 4 courses, €25. Wine €9–€30. Plus VAT at 7%. Restaurant 9km.
Closed	Rarely.
Directions	From Burgos N-623 for Santander. North of Quintanilla de Escalada, at km66 marker, right for Gallejones. On for Villanueva Rampally. There, left for Arreba. Posada signed on right after 2.6km.

Ethical Collection: Environment; Food.
See page 211.

Price band: C

Javier Morala & Valvanera Rodríguez
Posada Molino del Canto,
Molino del Canto s/n, Barrio La Cuesta,
09146 Valle de Zamanzas, Burgos

Tel	+34 947 571368
Email	molinodelcanto@telefonica.net
Web	www.molinodelcanto.com

L'Ayalga Posada Ecológica

Abandon the car and take a train on the narrow-gauge railway to Infiesto. Or come by bus. Either way, if you let them know beforehand, Luis or Conchi will be there to meet you. A hospitable and caring couple, they've taken infinite care to restore their farmhouse using only non-contaminating materials. Sand provides sound insulation between floorboards and ceiling, and cleaning products are homemade, using borax and essential oils. Herbs scent the garden, two endangered Asturcón ponies, bred by Luis, graze quietly, and green slopes lead the eye to dramatic mountain profiles. The rooms are attractively unadorned – just simple white walls, plain wood, warm-coloured fabrics. Thanks to solar panels, showers have constant hot water; wooden beds are treated with natural oils and wear decent mattresses. Your hosts, who manage without staff, give 1% of their income from guests to charity, and if you long for a massage after your ramble, your children will be looked after – you may even find them harvesting watermelons for lunch… Simplicity, hospitality and tranquillity.

Price	€49. Singles €43. Plus VAT at 7%.
Rooms	5 twins/doubles.
Meals	Vegetarian dinner €13. Plus VAT at 7%. Wine €6-€12.20.
Closed	21 December-8 January.
Directions	From Santander/Bilbao on A-8; exit 326 for Ribadesella/Arriondas. At r'bout, exit N-634 for Arriondas. At km361, towards Infiesto; then AS-254 for Campo de Caso. After 3km, left for La Pandiella. Or bus/train to Infiesto for pick up.

Luis A Díaz & Conchi de la Iglesia
L'Ayalga Posada Ecológica,
La Pandiella s/n,
33537 Piloña, Asturias

Mobile	+34 616 897638
Email	layalga@terrae.net
Web	www.terrae.net/layalga

Ethical Collection: Environment;
Community.
See page 211.

Price band: B

Hotel Posada del Valle

After two years spent searching the hills and valleys of Asturias, your green-minded hosts found the home of their dreams – a century-old farmhouse (now with solar panels) just inland from the rugged north coast, with sensational views to mountain, hill and meadow. Find a seat in hillside garden and gaze! Now they are nurturing new life from the soil – theirs is a fully registered organic farm – while running this small and beguiling Asturian hotel with its English feel. The apple orchard has matured, the sheep munch the hillside, the menu celebrates the best of things local and organic. Bedrooms, sensitively converted, are seductive affairs with shutters and old beams, polished wooden floors, exposed stone, colourful modern fabrics and washed walls to match. There's a stylishly uncluttered living room with an open brick fire, and a dining room with more views. You are close to the soaring Picos, the little-known sandy beaches of the Cantabrian coast and some of the most exceptional wildlife in Europe. Nigel and Joann have compiled well-researched notes on self-guided walks. *Hotel's annual fiesta supports local communities and artisans.*

Price	€62–€86. Singles €49.60–€60.
Rooms	12: 10 twins/doubles, 2 triples.
Meals	Breakfast €8. Dinner €23. Wine from €10.60.
Closed	Early November to late March.
Directions	N-634 Arriondas; AS-260 for Mirador del Fito. After 1km, right for Collia. Through village (don't turn to Ribadesella). Hotel 300m on left after village.

Ethical Collection: Environment; Community; Food. See page 211.

Price band: C

Nigel & Joann Burch
Hotel Posada del Valle,
Collia, 33549 Arriondas,
Asturias

Tel	+34 985 841157
Email	hotel@posadadelvalle.com
Web	www.posadadelvalle.com

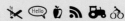

Posada Magoría

This very special 1920s house in the lee of the church has been carefully restored. Cool in summer, warm in winter, the pale interior is finely furnished and the top-floor bedrooms are elegantly sober, with magical views. New mattresses dress 1920s beds; shower rooms have glass-brick walls. But the heart of the place is the dining area where a huge rock juts into the room beside the long convivial table and the full-length wall tapestry lends the space weight. Here you are served organic and vegetarian soups, salads, cheeses, homemade bread and lashings of cider, while breakfasts are a purifying selection of muesli, cereals and mountain honey. Enrique has an intimate knowledge of this undiscovered region and his impassioned protest against a pipeline prompted its diversion. Woodland bears and bearded vultures, white-backed woodpeckers, orchids and irises sing their thanks. There's walking, mushroom-picking, advanced yoga... make a trip to this peaceful, remote, deeply serene place. The garden shares its walls with the ramparts, the fortified village is a gem. *Ask about music courses.*

Price	€45–€55. VAT included.
Rooms	6 twins/doubles.
Meals	Breakfast €6. Dinner €14. Wine €6–€20. VAT included.
Closed	Rarely.
Directions	Pamplona-Jaca N-240. Left at Berdun on HU-202 to Ansó. Here, 2nd left into village past mill; left along narrow street to church; last house on right. Steep walk from car park: unload at house first.

Enrique Ipas & Teresa Garayoa
Posada Magoría,
c/Milagro 32,
22728 Ansó, Huesca
Tel   +34 974 370049
Email   posadamagoria@gmail.com
Web   www.posadamagoria.com

Ethical Collection: Environment; Food.
See page 211.

Price band: C

Entry 137   Map 5

Casa Pio

Against a backdrop of craggy hills and olive fields is this sweet stone farmhouse and eco-friendly home. Home improvement experts from their barge life in Bristol, Philippa and Iain have done it all magnificently, using reclaimed wood and lots of imagination. The cosy little apartment hugs the house, its sunny courtyard entrance flanked by shuttered windows. Don't expect five-star comforts, just a kitchen/living room simply painted in white and shades of blue, a lovely snug bedroom to one side, a sofabed for kids and a shower room that sparkles. Riches are found here on a simple scale: pickings from the organic kitchen garden, the star of the show (you pay when you leave), and fresh eggs from the hens. Dog and cats doze, chickens roam, sun and wind provide the energy, a swimming pool asks for a splash in the sun. Wild flowers pepper the grounds, olive trees are harvested for oil. It's fun, simple, wholesome, homespun – life lived happily in the slow lane. You're five minutes from fishing on the Ebro, 20 from the beach and Tarragona's Roman ruins are under an hour's drive. Lovely. *Minimum stay two nights.*

Price	€50–€60 for 2 (€250–€650 per week).
Rooms	Apartment for 2-6.
Meals	Dinner €25 with wine. By arrangement (Fri or Sat only).
Closed	Rarely.
Directions	From Barcelona C32 & A-7 Tarragona & Reus. junc. 39 then N340 El Perello. Right onto TV3022. At km12.5 marker, left onto track. House 200m on right.

Ethical Collection: Environment; Food.
See page 211.

Price band: C

Philippa Bungard
Casa Pio,
Polygon 13, Parcela 46-47,
43513 Rasquera, Tarragona

Tel	+34 977 265208
Email	philbungard@yahoo.co.uk

Refugio Marnes

A shepherd's refuge and a Bedouin tent in a valley ringed by mountains. This is for those who demand off the beaten track; dozens of paths to explore but none are signed – not even on the map! Dutch Willem and Richard bought both finca and forested land several years ago. With no mains power or utilities – still none – and an intermittent water supply, modernising was a challenge. They've done it all themselves, brilliantly, in cool eco style. From the parking area it's a 200m walk down a steep donkey track to the cottage and tent. La Ruina is cosy, compact and simply stylish, with a mezzanine for an extra bed and a private terrace. La Jaima, 100m away – a structure tried and tested by nomadic tribes for two millennia – is huge, theatrical and great fun, with modern plumbing and solar-generated electricity. Outside, a hammock swings from the branch of an ancient tree; the shared pool is unfenced and – delicious. You're utterly remote here, though the owners are unobtrusively available. The night skies are the clearest you're ever likely to see.

Price	La Ruina €341-€694. La Jaima (tent) €418-€588. Prices per week. B&B €90 per night.
Rooms	Cottage for 2-4. Bedouin tent for 2-4.
Meals	Breakfast €9.50, by arrangement. Restaurant 5-minute drive.
Closed	La Jaima: October-March.
Directions	AP-7/E15 exit 63; thro' Benissa on N-332 for Calpe. After Benissa, right on CV-750; left fork onto CV-749, signed Pinos. On for 1km, over little blue bridge; immediately right up steep hill. Signed.

Willem Pieffers
Refugio Marnes,
Pda Marnes 20115,
03720 Benissa, Alicante

Mobile	+34 637 063003
Email	info@refugiomarnes.com
Web	www.refugiomarnes.com

Ethical Collection: Environment.
See page 211.

Price band: C

Cortijada Los Gazquez

The Beckmanns have joyfully restored five houses that make up this cortijada. The ceilings are lofty, the finish is perfect, the thinking is environmental, the family is delightful. There's Simon, artist and designer, Donna, illustrator, Solomon and Sesame, twins; they are completely dedicated to their restored family house and cannot wait to cook for and entertain their guests. Rooms were unfinished at the time of our visit but promise to be warm, simple and light, with a fun/funky twist. Olive oil soaps sit by cool concrete basins, pine logs furnish roaring fires, rainwater is harvested, and wind and solar power keep floors toasty and water piping hot. Reed beds eliminate impurities and the water irrigates the land; soon there will be a natural pool and a wood-fired sauna. And the landscape? The farmhouse sits magnificently and remotely in the national park surrounded by fruit, almond and olive trees... the view of La Sagra mountain is beautiful in every weather. Ramblers, artists, nature lovers will be happy here. All you hear is the call of the eagle and the owl at dusk. *Minimum stay two nights.*

Ethical Collection: Environment;
Community; Food.
See page 211.

Price band: C

Price	€85.
Rooms	6: 3 twins/doubles, 3 doubles.
Meals	Dinner with wine, €18.
Closed	Christmas.
Directions	At Velez Blanco Visitors Centre (signed) 1st right, signed Las Almahollas. Left at fork, follow road for 8km. At junc. follow signs to Los Gazquez.

Simon & Donna Beckmann
Cortijada Los Gazquez,
Hoya de Carrascal,
04830 Velez Blanco, Almería

Tel	+44 (0)20 7193 6056
Email	info@losgazquez.com
Web	www.losgazquez.com

Casa Rural El Paraje

A short track through wildlife-filled groves of almond, chestnut, olive and oak brings you to this old farmhouse. From the terrace – originally the threshing circle – stretch glorious views and all around is superb walking country: one of the reasons Anita and Walter chose to settle here. They're Dutch but completely at home in their adopted country; they spent many years exploring Spain and know it intimately. They are now experts on the sierra, will advise on walking and lend you maps and mountain bikes. Their organically run farm covers about 20 hectares but the house was semi-derelict and they did much of the restoration themselves. The bedrooms are beautifully simple, with original dark wooden shutters, sparkling white bathrooms and underfloor heating powered by solar thermals – a boon in the Alpujarran winter. Downstairs is a small bar and restaurant and the food is a treat: Walter uses fruits, vegetables and herbs from the kitchen garden to delicious effect and serves local wines. He and Anita are the kindest, friendliest hosts and the area is refreshingly tourist-free. Great place, great value!

Price	€48. Apartment €60 (€360 per week).
Rooms	4 + 1: 3 twins/doubles; 1 twin/double with separate bath. 1 apartment for 2-3.
Meals	Breakfast €4.50. Dinner, 3 courses, €15. Wine €6-€15. Restaurant 2km.
Closed	Rarely.
Directions	From Málaga, east on N-340. Pass Motril, then left on N-345 to Albuñol & Cádiar. Then A-4127 for Mecina; left on A-4130 to Bérchules. Here, at crossing, left for Trévelez. After 2km, right at sign.

Anita Beijer & Walter Michels
Casa Rural El Paraje,
Ctra. Granada-Bérchules s/n,
18451 Bérchules, Granada

Tel	+34 958 064029
Email	info@elparaje.com
Web	www.elparaje.com

Ethical Collection: Environment; Food.
See page 211.

Price band: B

Finca La Herradura

The tarmac road ends (along with water, electricity and sewage connections) and the bumpy climb begins, up and away into the Alpujarras to reach the Finca – a low-slung set of stone peasant buildings among ancient, terraced olive groves, hemmed in on all sides by a natural coliseum of near-vertical slopes. It's hard to find fault with the environmental credentials of Jeanette and Russell's rustic, genuinely 'off grid' Finca: lighting in the two comfortable, low-key casitas is solar; the interiors are sweetly decked in local furniture (including a lovely eucalyptus bed); paints are natural mineral washes; water is from the spring. Stones from the river that runs below the house are used inside and out, and they have stuck doggedly to the local recipe for the ceilings, made from river reed (dehusked by hand) and waterproofed with clay. Everything has been done on a shoestring, by hand and with only a modicum of help from a local builder. Birds chirrup, goat bells jingle, the pool is delicious, the terraces are spectacular and the night skies shine. *B&B available September-March.*

Price	£360-£535 (sterling) per week.
Rooms	Casita for 2. Apartment for 2.
Meals	Dinner, by arrangement, €15 (mainly vegetarian).
Closed	Never.
Directions	From Orgiva GR4202 Tijola road for approx. 5km. Follow unmade track for 3km; right by big signed stone.

Ethical Collection: Environment.
See page 211.

Price band: C

Jeanette & Russell Welham
Finca La Herradura,
Buzon 93 Carretera de Tijola,
18418 Orgiva, Granada

Tel	+34 690 264186
Email	fincalaherradura@hotmail.com
Web	www.fincalaherraduraretreat.iowners.net

Entry 142   Map 5

El Cielo de Cáñar

The road climbs up, the ground falls away until, suddenly, somewhere between the earth and the sky, you've arrived... this low-lying, Alpujarran slate cortijo seems to grow out of the stony southern slopes of the Sierra Nevada on which it is perched. The view is vast: Alpujarra mountains, white villages, Orgiva. Energy comes from the sun, water from the Sierra. Each bedroom, opening onto a private terrace, shares the panorama. Interiors are sharp and clean-cut (like the air) with a mostly white colour scheme that is spiked with bright Indian fabrics, Moroccan lampshades, modern art. Bathrooms are crisply contemporary. Simply chic, yet cool and restful, this is a place to recharge batteries. No TVs, no phones, just a spacious, terraced garden with a bounteous orchard, large pool and private corners to read or snooze. Feeling active? Hiking and riding are on the doorstep, Granada and the beach are an hour away. Return to excellent home-produced dinners, and stargazing from the terrace. Well-travelled English owners John and Orna fell in love with the area and now they happily share it.

Price	From €97. Price for whole house (sleeps 14) on application.
Rooms	5 doubles. Whole house available for self-catering.
Meals	Dinner €24, by arrangement. Wine from €8.
Closed	Rarely.
Directions	A-44 from Granada or coast to Lanjarón & Órgiva. At Órgiva, A-4132 dir. Bubion & left at GR-4201 to Cañar. At Bar Piqui, hard left & follow road for 2km up hill to El Cielo de Cañar.

Orna Gorman
El Cielo de Cáñar,
Llano de Manzano 001,
18418 Cáñar, Granada

Tel	+34 958 953015
Email	enquiries@elcielodecanar.com
Web	www.elcielodecanar.com

Ethical Collection: Environment; Food. See page 211.

Price band: C

Entry 143   Map 5

Los Piedaos

At the end of the long winding track, on a tree-covered ridge beneath the soaring Sierra Nevada, the multi-levelled farmstead has been renovated by its "organic" architect owner with shade, privacy and huge views in mind. Each white casita reveals old tiles and timbers, recycled shutters and doors and a colourful hotch-potch of terraces and furnishings: convivial dining tables, throws over sofas, simple bedrooms/bathrooms and plenty of novels. The owners – keen hispanophiles, welcoming but discreet – are passionate about the organic growth of the Orgiva area and are aiming for absolute sustainability. Roofs are painted white to reflect sunlight, grey water is channelled into pretty gardens, hot water comes from solar panels, the pools are cleansed by copper/silver purification, air conditioning is low energy, olives and oranges are organically grown. Trails lead to quiet spots, swallows swoop above ancient olives and a 40-minute walk brings you to popular Orgiva, one of Spain's hippy towns (yoga, tai chi, meditation). Exceptional peace, subtle architecture, soaring views.

Price	€400–€860 per week.
Rooms	4 casitas: 3 for 4, 1 for 2-3.
Meals	Restaurants in Orgiva, 3km.
Closed	Rarely.
Directions	Detailed directions & map on website.

Ethical Collection: Environment.
See page 211.

Price band: C

Shujata & David Dry
Los Piedaos,
Las Barreras,
8400 Órgiva, Granada

Tel	+34 958 763492
Email	holidays@lospiedaos.com
Web	www.holidays-in-southern-spain.com

Fountainhead

One of the hippest hotels to open in recent years, and one of the most sensitive to its surroundings. A preservation philosophy clings lovingly to everything: unadulterated olive groves and almond trees, solar-soaked flat roofs powering hot water, grey water feeding the garden. Fountainhead surveys Andalucía at its wildest – 15 miles from Málaga, Sierra de Caramolos behind. A carob tree marks your entry onto the walled patio where a circular hole in the wall portals the cane-covered walkway to your vibrant casita, bordered by wild flowers and trim cacti. The casitas have been conceived with zen-like lines that belie Helen's fiesta of designer-savvy touches and glorious patterns. The fridge is packed full of goodies from Manchego cheese to strawberries; croissants and bread are delivered to your door. Architects by trade, Helen and Peter are your thoughtful hosts, zealous about organics and up for a laugh. They now produce their own olive oil, vegetables and almonds. Unsurprisingly, the menu is local sophistication par excellence with staples of lemon grass and cumin soup and a salad of langoustine, orange and chicory.

Price	€225.
Rooms	4 suites.
Meals	Dinner €30. Wine from €12. Restaurant 15-minute drive.
Closed	Mid-November to mid-December.
Directions	Directions on booking.

Helen Bartlett & Peter Jewkes
Fountainhead, Partido del Río el Terral,
Fuente la Camacha,
29180 Riogordo, Málaga

Mobile	+34 696 183309
Email	info@fountainheadinspain.com
Web	www.fountainheadinspain.com

Ethical Collection: Environment; Food.
See page 211.

Price band: E

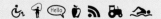

Fuegoblanco

This true Andaluz finca (half 1950s, half new – fully organic) sits in its own nascent citrus grove, relishing the fruit-ripening sun that illuminates every corner of the house. Kenneth clearly saw the light by choosing the giant windows to embolden the entrance hallway and the large shared sitting room downstairs – a great space to be cool in in summer (or snug by the wood-burner) and an excellent reference library to plan hikes. Otherwise, in a child-friendly garden, ruminate in a swing seat among the olive trees. Simply furnished in pine, with Indian hangings and Casablanca fans, each bedroom has its own spotless if slightly spartan bathroom with solar-heated water and guests have their own entrance to the main house. Outside is lovely, dining at pretty individual tables on the patio, enjoying speciality vegetarian dishes or homemade Seville orange marmalade for breakfast. Above the house, the pool is a splendid place to flop amidst plants, bougainvillea and hillside views; similarly recline on rough-hewn wooden furniture that the very first lemon sale kindly provided.

Price	€73–€83. Singles €48–€53. Suite €100–€122.
Rooms	6: 2 doubles, 2 twins, 1 single, 1 suite.
Meals	Lunch €7.50. Dinner, 3 courses with wine, €22.50. Restaurants 5-min drive.
Closed	Rarely.
Directions	A357 from Malaga, right to Alora; 2nd r'bout exit El Chorro; signed 2km on right.

Ethical Collection: Environment; Food.
See page 211.

Price band: C

Kenneth & Sarah Beachill
Fuegoblanco,
Partido los Aneales,
29500 Álora, Málaga

Tel	+34 952 497439
Email	enquiries@fuegoblanco.com
Web	www.fuegoblanco.com

Andalucia Yurts

Few places sit in such natural seclusion – astonishing that you are only ten miles from the Costa del Sol. Sited by a river so clean you can drink from it (with otters and wild boar as fellow guests), the place is engulfed by cork and pine plantations to a backdrop of sheer soaring peaks. With only one building in sight – the castle in Gaucín – it is the sort of wild escape nature lovers adore. The B&B centres on a pretty cottage, sensitively restored using old wooden beams and sustainable materials. Its nerve centre is the veranda, which is covered in long concrete benches, comfortably decked in exotic Indian fabrics. Your bedrooms are under canvas, but don't worry – these two yurts are spacious, airy and utterly private, tucked away in different corners of the smallholding. The Hoggs – tree surgeons by trade – are engaging people, and passionate about the environment. Fellow guests may include yogis, birdwatchers and writers. As well as being an organic farm, water is pumped from the river and solar panels are de rigeur. The African Bush comes to Spain – hurrah!

Price	€35 p.p.
Rooms	2 yurts for 2-4.
Meals	Dinner with wine, €20.
Closed	November-March.
Directions	A-377 from Manilva to Gaucín. At km21 marker, right after bridge. Follow track for 3.8km; 2nd right is La Huerta.

Penny Hogg
Andalucia Yurts,
La Huerta,
29480 Gaucín, Málaga
Tel   +34 952 117486
Email hoggs@vsatmail.com
Web   www.andaluciayurts.com

Ethical Collection: Environment.
See page 211.

Price band: C

The Hoopoe Yurt Hotel

Under the shade of cork and olive trees, these authentic Mongolian, Afghani and Maimani yurts sit in splendid Andalucían isolation. On raised wooden platforms, the felt-lined white circular tents are reinforced with arching roof poles that support a domed crown, while wicker baskets, ethnic furniture, sheepskin rugs and bold colours create a rustic but romantic mood: the charming and well-travelled young owners have made the yurts stylish while maintaining a 'back to nature' feel. There's a compost loo and solar-heated water in the bamboo-walled shower rooms; indeed, the whole camp is run on solar power. Wonderful views of the soaring mountains may be enjoyed from a hammock slung between two cork trees or on a bamboo sun bed beside the freshwater pool. The staff are wonderful, massage is possible and once a week there's a film screening outdoors. Wake to birdsong, cowbells and the distant rumble of trains; at night, tiptoe your way to bed past twinkling lights in the trees. Henrietta uses the best local and organic ingredients and the food is delicious. The whitewashed village is a 20-minute walk. Bliss.

Price	€130.
Rooms	5 yurts for 2, each with shower.
Meals	Sandwiches/paninis €5. Dinner with wine, €30.
Closed	Mid-October to end April.
Directions	After Benaojan, cont. for C. de la Frontera; there, 1st left after fountain. Before petrol station, left on track, then left at fork; after 1km, right onto track before white house.

Ethical Collection: Environment; Food.
See page 211.

Price band: D

Ed & Henrietta Hunt
The Hoopoe Yurt Hotel,
Apartado de Correos 23,
29380 Cortes de la Frontera, Málaga

Tel	+34 951 168040
Email	info@yurthotel.com
Web	www.yurthotel.com

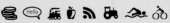

El Sueño

When summer hits Andalucia's 'Coast of Light', here's a cool, eco-chic country retreat 15 minutes inland, near whitewashed Vejer de la Frontera. On eight acres of chemical-free soil – where permaculture prevails amidst a wet woodland conservation area teeming with nature – are three white open-plan casitas powered by a local wind turbine. Expect cool terracotta floors, warm wood stoves, bright kitchen tiles under high ceilings, a shared fenced bio-pool and everything to keep children happy. If you're a big party, rent the cortijo close by, luxurious with its sitting rooms, four-poster beds, double-ended baths and private infinity pool. Barbecue in the shade of trees and climbing vines, stroll the Citrus Walk, enjoy the heady scent of the ornamental herb gardens; the big house has its own bar, terrace and pool-with-views. Pergolas are of sustainable local pine, all water is harvested or comes from the wells, and grey water replenishes orchards and trees. Sean and Tanya, inspiring stewards of their land, are friendly and enthusiastic; ask about childminding, catering and more. Dreamy.

Price	Casitas €395–€1,375. House €1,250–€2,750. Prices per week.
Rooms	3 casitas: 1 for 2; 1 for 4; 1 for 6. House for 8 (2 doubles, 2 twins).
Meals	Restaurants 500m.
Closed	Rarely.
Directions	From Vejer, N-340 direction Tarifa; at km41 marker, right signed El Soto; after 250m, left into village. House on right, after 500m.

Sean & Tanya Macrae
El Sueño,
El Soto 64,
11150 Vejer de la Frontera, Cádiz
Tel   +34 956 450240
Email   relax@elsueno.net
Web   www.elsueno.net

Ethical Collection: Environment.
See page 211.

Price band: C

Can Marti Agroturismo

Only the tinkling of bells from the neighbour's sheep breaks the silence in this tranquil wooded valley — and the occasional bray from the two donkeys. A far cry indeed from the crowds of Ibiza. Peter and Isabelle have breathed organic life back into the gently sloping terraced land. Olive, fig, almond and carob trees have been revived, fruit and vegetables planted and the old stone farmhouse has been naturally limewashed and transformed into rustic but immaculate guest apartments. Simple, colourful rooms are designed in the traditional Ibicencan way (rainwater is collected from the roof for regional irrigation) with a touch of the contemporary (photovolaic and solar thermal panels). There are juniper-beamed ceilings, thick walls, and thoughtfully equipped kitchens. The Brantschens' passion for travel informs the different cultural themes: Moroccan mirrors, an antique Indian staircase, a French sink, Mexican pots. Delicious organic breakfasts, with homemade breads and jams and fresh orange juice in season, may be brought to your terrace each morning. *Farm shop on site.*

Price	€120–€160. Cottage €200–€250. Prices per night.
Rooms	3 studios/apartments for 2. Extra beds available. 1 cottage for 4.
Meals	Breakfast €12. Restaurants 10-minute walk.
Closed	15 October to end March.
Directions	On Ibiza-Sant Joan road, just after turn to Portinatx, right to Can Marti, signed; house 900m up track. Or, bus from Ibiza to Sant Joan (20km) twice a day; owners will arrange for pick up.

Ethical Collection: Environment; Food.
See page 211.

Price band: D

Peter Brantschen
Can Marti Agroturismo,
Venda de las Ripolls 29,
07810 Sant Joan de Labritja, Ibiza

Tel	+34 971 333500
Email	info@canmarti.com
Web	www.canmarti.com

Casa Amatista

Rest mind and body in this delightful retreat of cottage apartments and one Mongolian yurt. Warm, hospitable Daniel and Zanna are passionate about sustainable living, and all is recycled and composted. Showers are solar-heated and waste water is filtered for the garden. And what a garden! An oasis of exuberant greenery in Lanzarote's arid landscape, it bursts with flowering shrubs, organic fruit trees and aloe vera, in amazing contrast to volcanic nooks and crannies. Laze around the pretty solar-heated pool (there's a sofa in the shade) or climb to the sun deck for views of the still-rumbling Timanfaya volcano. Each light and airy open-plan apartment is different, with a simple kitchen, a compact shower room, a private terrace. Happy colours reflect Zanna's personal touch: prints, wall hangings, rugs, a splash of lime green or fuchsia. In the wood-floored Group Room, join in yoga or weekly meditation sessions; there are alternative therapies too. Wagging Bonnie likes to be walked; nearby beaches lure surfers and sunbathers; nature lovers will find plenty to explore. Remote, peaceful, lovely.

Price	Cottage €110-€120. Studio & casitas €60-€80. Yurt €60.
Rooms	Cottage for 6. Studio for 2. 3 casitas for 2. Yurt for 2.
Meals	Restaurant 2km.
Closed	Never.
Directions	From airport LZ-2 to Arrecife. LZ-20 thro' San Bartolomé; at r'bout 2nd exit to Mozaga. At r'bout 3rd exit to La Vegueta. At x-roads left to Mancha Blanca; left by pink house onto Camino de las Huertitas. Right after 400m (signed); on left.

Daniel Jacobi & Zanna Barge
Casa Amatista,
Camino las Huertitas 11,
35560 La Vegueta-Tinajo, Lanzarote
Tel   +34 928 840867
Email   info@villa-amatista.com
Web   www.villa-amatista.com

Ethical Collection: Environment.
See page 211.

Price band: C

La Miniera

Take a ferrous mountainside, add old mine spoil, mix with some ancient dark diorite stone quarried to exhaustion and you might expect a barren landscape of nothingness. And yet, sitting on top, is an oasis of biodiversity. The Anaus have won an award for this miraculous recovery, and their 40 acres are filled with plants, trees and wildlife – all surrounding a once-derelict mine headquarters, now an unusual B&B. Every corner of the hardened terrain is newly cultivated to feed guests – and wild creatures; just-picked ingredients along with wild fungi and berries are used in seasonal menus based on traditional Jewish-Italian recipes. Expert Roberta has written recipe books, and can feed up to 30. Energy is hydro-powered and felled wood warms the bedrooms, simply decorated with old-fashioned "grandmother's furniture"; the small house, basic but heated and with an open fire, is for self-caterers. They have also created an on-site museum exploring the history of the mine, there are shady terraces with deckchairs, ruins to explore and mule tracks that go back to Napoleonic times. Unique.

Price	€74. Cottage €500 per week.
Rooms	3 + 1: 1 double, 1 triple, 1 quadruple. Cottage for 2-3 + cot.
Meals	Breakfast €8–€14. Dinner €24–€35. Wine from €6.
Closed	Rarely.
Directions	From Ivrea to Lessolo for 6km. Ignore 1st sign for Lessolo, on for 1.5km, left for Calea. Signed up to green iron gates.

Ethical Collection: Environment; Food.
See page 211.

Price band: C

Roberta Anau
La Miniera,
via Miniere 9, Calea,
10010 Lessolo

Tel	+39 0125 58618
Email	roberta@laminiera.it
Web	www.laminiera.it

Agriturismo Cervano B&B

Surrounded by wild orchids and violets at the highest point of the garden, the sun splashing colour across the sky as it sets over majestic Lake Garda, you could be fooled into believing you were a 19th-century wine merchant returning from Milan for the harvest of your country estate. What a pleasant surprise you would have on entering your house if that were true. Anna and Gino have mastered the restoration of Gino's once-crumbling family home, a fine example of Lombard 'fort' design, and the interior is stylish and contemporary: bathrooms are slick Italian, new beds are dressed in handmade linen. Despite the modernity, Anna and Gino have constantly kept the 1800s in mind – only the insulated roof did not belong to the original plot: exposed beams have been perfectly restored, floors imitate the original style and the marble breakfast bar is Verona's most rare: speckled pink and red. Wine is still produced on site but now it's organic; solar panels heat water; a ground pump heats the house. The apartments, with their own stylish kitchens, are also a tribute to restoration genius. *Minimum stay three nights.*

Price	€100–€150. Whole house (sleeps 7-8) €500–€900. Apt for 4, €110–€130 (€15 per extra person). Apt for 10, €150–€300 p.p.
Rooms	3 + 2: 1 double, 1 double & sofabed, 1 triple. Whole house available for self-catering. 1 apartment for 4, 1 for 10.
Meals	Restaurant 1km.
Closed	Never.
Directions	From Gargnano, right towards golf club. Signed.

Gino & Anna Massarani
Agriturismo Cervano B&B,
via Cervano 14,
25088 Toscolano Maderno

Tel   +39 0365 548398
Email   info@cervano.com
Web   www.cervano.com

Ethical Collection: Environment; Food.
See page 211.

Price band: D

Tenuta Le Sorgive – Le Volpi Agriturismo

This 19th-century farmhouse, on a 28 organic-hectare farm, has been in the family for two generations; it has a distinct community feel as visionary Vittorio, head of the family and eco tour guide-in-chief, leads future generations into soulful sustainability. The heating is fuelled by homemade chippings with a biomass boiler lending a hand; solar panels absorb the sunshine to light the rooms... even the wild animals and birds are attracted by his green methods (he plants prunes just for them). A great place to bring children of all ages: visit the horses, cycle, use the gym, swim in the pool. There's archery here and go-karting and watersporting at Lake Garda. The farmhouse, crowned with a pierced dovecote, flanked by a carriage house and stables, remains impressive, even if some character has been lost during restoration. Big guest rooms with wooden rafters are a mix of old and new. Some have attractive metalwork beds, others a balcony, two have a mezzanine with beds for the children. Vittorio's sister Anna runs the Le Volpi taverna close by. *Minimum stay three nights in high season.*

Price	€85–€105.
	Apartments €550–€900 per week.
Rooms	8 + 2: 8 twins/doubles.
	2 apartments for 4.
Meals	Breakfast €5 for self-caterers. Dinner with wine, €15–€28. Restaurant closed January & Mon/Tues evenings.
Closed	Never.
Directions	Exit A4 Milano-Venezia at Desenzano for Castiglione delle Stiviere; left at traffic lights; left after 20m to Solferino. At x-roads, left. Signed.

Ethical Collection: Environment.
See page 211.

Price band: C

Signor Vittorio Serenelli
Tenuta Le Sorgive – Le Volpi Agriturismo,
via Piridello 6,
46040 Solferino

Tel	+39 0376 854252
Email	info@lesorgive.it
Web	www.lesorgive.it

Ca' del Rocolo

Such an undemanding, delightful place to be and such a warm, enthusiastic young family to be with. Maurizio ran a restaurant in Verona, Ilaria was a journalist and has three cookbooks to her name; they gave it all up for a country life for their children. Their 1800s farmhouse is on the side of a hill at the end of a long track overlooking forested hills and the vast Lessinia National Park. Over a decade has passed since their move; Maurizio did much of the "bio" renovation himself and the result is authentic and attractive. Simple cotton rugs cover stripped bedroom floors, rough plaster walls are whitewashed, rooms are big and airy – with local country furniture and excellent beds – and baths are heated by solar-thermals. There's also a shared kitchen. Breakfasts are at the long farmhouse table or out on the terrace, making the most of the views: delicious food, seasonal cakes, home-grown fruits, happy conversation. Dinner, mostly vegetarian, is an occasional affair. This is a seven-hectare all-organic farm, with olives and fruit trees, hens, horses and industriously tended beehives.

Price	€63–€70 (€410–€450 per week).
Rooms	3: 2 doubles, 1 family room.
Meals	Light meal €15. Wine €15. Shared guest kitchen. Restaurant 4km.
Closed	Rarely.
Directions	Directions on booking.

Ilaria & Maurizio Corazza
Ca' del Rocolo,
via Gaspari 3,
loc. Quinto, 37142 Verona

Tel   +39 0458 700879
Email   info@cadelrocolo.com
Web   www.cadelrocolo.com

Ethical Collection: Environment; Food.
See page 211.

Price band: C

Entry 155   Map 6

Agriturismo La Faula

An exuberant miscellany of dogs, donkeys and peacocks on a modern, working farm where rural laissez-faire and eco mindedness seamlessly mingle. La Faula has been in Luca's family for years; he and Paul, young and dynamic, abandoned the city to find themselves working harder than ever – reforesting over-grazed fields, creating creature-friendly woodlands, opening springs for migrating birds. They have put much enthusiasm into their wine business, organic farm and local community – and there's plenty over for guests. The house stands in gentle countryside at the base of the Julian Alps – a big and comfortable home. Each bedroom is delightful, furniture is old, bathrooms are new. There is a bistro-style restaurant where home-reared produce is served and an enormous old pergola provides dappled shade during the day. Sit and dream awhile with a glass of estate wine next to the pool (the overflow feeds the garden) or wander round the vineyard and watch the work in progress. You'll be recommending La Faula to your friends: it's superb on every level. And perfect for families. *Minimum stay two nights.*

Price	€80. Apartments €455 per week.
Rooms	9 + 4: 9 twins/doubles. 4 studio apartments for 2-4.
Meals	Dinner €18. Wine €15. Restaurant 500m.
Closed	16 September-14 March.
Directions	A23 exit Udine Nord dir. Tarvisio & Tricesimo. From SS13 Pontebbana dir. Povoletto-Cividale. At r'bout, right dir. Povoletto. At Ravosa, pass Trattoria Al Sole on left; right after 20m. Signed.

Ethical Collection: Environment; Community; Food.
See page 211.

Price band: C

Paul Mackay & Luca Colautti
Agriturismo La Faula,
via Faula 5,
Ravosa di Povoletto,
33040 Udine

Mobile	+39 334 3996734
Web	www.faula.com

Agriturismo Giandriale

Once city dwellers in Milan, Giani and Lucia have made the restoration of what was a dilapidated property their life's work. On top of the world, the house is isolated but the surroundings are heavenly: high pastures dotted with trees, dense woods beyond, Alpine views. The Val di Vara is a completely protected environmental zone, where hunting is forbidden and only organic farming allowed. Join in with the farm activities if you wish, or doze off and dream; the pleasures are simple. Bedrooms are too (no hanging space). Some in the house, some in the outbuildings, all are solar-heated; thick stone walls, colourful rugs, cane and bamboo, and old chestnut furniture alongside modern. Your hosts have young children who are happy to meet yours – there's so much space to run around in, and Lucia helps children identify flowers, trees and wildlife. There's even an adventure park in the trees. Breakfasts are sociable affairs around the big table, a feast of home-grown, home-reared produce. Beware the rough and narrow track, leave the low-slung Morgan behind! Tranquillity is your reward.

Price	€70–€80. Apartments €40–€45 per person per night.
Rooms	5 + 2: 2 doubles, 3 triples. 2 apartments: 1 for 4, 1 for 5.
Meals	Breakfast for self-caterers included. Dinner €20. Wine €5-€10.
Closed	Rarely.
Directions	From Sestri Levante, N523 for Parma. On for 14km thro' tunnel & immed. right, before 'Torza', for Tavarone then Giandriale. Steep, pot-holed track to top.

Giani & Lucia Nereo
Agriturismo Giandriale,
loc. Giandriale 5,
19010 Tavarone di Maissana

Tel	+39 0187 840279
Email	info@giandriale.it
Web	www.giandriale.it

Ethical Collection: Environment.
See page 211.

Price band: C

Fattoria Barbialla Nuova

A 500-hectare organic farm specialising in white Chianina cattle, fragrant olive oil and white truffles. Guido, Gianluca and Marco have worked hard to provide somewhere stylish, beautiful and bio-sensitive to stay on this glorious nature reserve. There are three farmhouses here, all with sweeping views, all on the top of a hill. The largest, 'Le Trosce' (sleeps eight), is all on one floor but has several levels. 'Doderi' is divided into three apartments, simple and minimalist, with joyous bedcovers and 60s-style furniture for stylishness, originality and colour. The apartments in 'Brentina', deeper in the woods, are a touch more rustic, though designers will love the simplicity of the whitewashed walls and the handmade staircase; all have delicious bathrooms and hot water courtesy of the Tuscan sun. Outside are pergolas, patios and pools, chic with deckchairs and decking, and an orchard and hens. Marco or Guido is always around to help, and the autumn is the time to go if you fancy a spot of truffle-hunting, accompanied by an expert and his dog. *Minimum stay seven nights in high season.*

Price	Apts for 2, €420–€570. Apts for 4, €680–€1,050. Apts for 6, €850–€1,320. Farmhouse €1,250–€2,000. Prices per week.
Rooms	7 apartments: 2 for 2, 3 for 4, 2 for 6. Farmhouse for 8.
Meals	Restaurant 3km.
Closed	10 January–10 March.
Directions	A1 exit Firenze/Scandicci, follow signs to 'S.G.C. FI-PI-LI' direction Pisa & exit San Miniato up hill to Montaione; 4km after Corazzano, on right opp. white 6km sign.

Ethical Collection: Environment; Food.
See page 211.

Price band: C

	Àrghilo Società Agricola
	Fattoria Barbialla Nuova,
	via Castastrada 49,
	50050 Montaione
Tel	+39 0571 677259
Email	info@barbiallanuova.it
Web	www.barbiallanuova.it

Locanda Casanuova

Ancient in spite of its name, Casanuova was once a monastery, then an orphanage, then a farmhouse… Ursula and Thierry took it on 20 years ago, rescuing the house and returning the land to organic use. They're a very generous couple – Ursula may invite you to join her at yoga – living in a locanda that exudes a serene simplicity. Meals are delicious, seasonal, sociable affairs in the lovely refectory, off which is a library where you can pore over trekking maps at a big round table… no TVs here! Bedrooms, peaceful, charming, furnished with natural fabrics and colours, have a serenely monastic air, while bathrooms are white and modern. As well as being a talented chef with a cookbook to her name, Ursula is an imaginative gardener; green secret corners, inviting terraces and unusual plants abound. Just a short walk from the house, in a clearing in the woods, is an enchanting swimming 'pond' – a natural, self-cleansing pool with lily pads, surrounded by decking. By the old mulberry tree 800m from the house are two pleasing apartments, one on the ground floor. *Certified organic chianti wine producers.*

Price	€90. Half-board €70 p.p. Apartments €75–€100.
Rooms	20: 12 doubles, 2 suites, 4 singles, 2 apartments (1 for 2, 1 for 4).
Meals	Dinner €25–€30. Wine €9–€35.
Closed	2 November–15 March.
Directions	A1 from Rome exit Incisa Valdarno. Follow signs to Figline, right for Brollo; left before Brollo for San Martino; on for 2km.

Ursula & Thierry Besançon
Locanda Casanuova,
San Martino Altoreggi 52,
50063 Figline Valdarno

Tel   +39 0559 500027
Email   locanda@casanuova-toscana.it
Web   www.casanuova.info

Ethical Collection: Food.
See page 211.

Price band: C

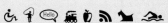

Entry 159   Map 6

Podere Salicotto

Watch sunsets fire the Tuscan hills; catch the sunrise as it brings the valleys alive. Views from this silent hilltop farmhouse roll off in every direction. Brunch – that most civilised meal – is a speciality at Salicotto, with produce from the organic farm and Silvia and Paolo, a well-travelled, warm and adventurous couple, happy for you to be as active or as idle as you like. Eat in the big farmhouse kitchen or under the pergola, as deer wander across the field below. Paolo is full of ideas and will take you sailing in a six-berth boat that has crossed the Atlantic – or organise wine-tasting and cycling trips. The beams-and-terracotta bedrooms are airy and welcoming, full of soft Tuscan colours and furnished with simplicity but care: antiques, monogrammed sheets, great showers heated by solar thermals, radiators warmed by a biomass boiler. B&B guests are in the main house (private entrance); the studio apartment is in the converted barn. Visit Siena, medieval Buonconvento, Tuscan hill towns. Return to a hammock and a laze around the pool, a glass of wine, a fabulous view. A treat to wake to every morning.

Ethical Collection: Environment; Food.
See page 211.

Price band: D

Price	B&B €150 (€980 per week). Studio €1,200 per week.
Rooms	6 + 1: 6 doubles. Studio for 2-4.
Meals	Breakfast for self-caterers, €15. Lunch or dinner with wine, €25, on request. Restaurants nearby.
Closed	Mid-November to mid-March.
Directions	From Siena via Cassia to Buonconvento. With the Consorzio Agrario on your left, turn immed. left; road to Podere on right.

Silvia Forni
Podere Salicotto,
Podere Salicotto 73,
53022 Buonconvento

Tel   +39 0577 809087
Email   info@poderesalicotto.com
Web   www.poderesalicotto.com

Montebelli Agriturismo & Country Hotel

Step outside and breathe in the scents of myrtle and juniper. Wander up to the ancient oak at the top of the hill and watch the sun set. And explore this whole lovely area on horseback: Montebelli has nine horses and three ponies (mountain bikes, too). Little tracks lead you past gnarled oaks and tall pines to vineyards, olive groves and a small lake. The farm, which has several solar panels, is run by a lovely family: Carla, her husband and their son Alessandro, back from a life in South Africa. Loungers line the elegant pool; jars of the farm's produce – honey, jam, olive oil, grappa and wine. The cooking is Tuscan/Neapolitan, the produce home-grown and organic, the quality outstanding. Cookery courses may be in the offing – do ask. Breakfast is served on the big, covered terrace; on a summer evening there could be a concert or a barbecue. Bedrooms are cool, clean and welcoming, their white walls, wooden floors, understated furnishings and interesting pictures. The new eco build is a success, striking the perfect note of simplicity in an unspoiled place. Superb value. *Spa on site.*

Price	€160–€240. Suites €200–€270.
Rooms	45 doubles, twins, triples & suites.
Meals	Dinner €37. Half board €25 extra p.p. Wine from €15.
Closed	January to March.
Directions	From SS1 exit Gavorrano Scalo for Ravi-Caldana; 5km, turn for Caldana. After 2.5km, sign for Montebelli.

Carla Filotico Tosi
Montebelli Agriturismo & Country Hotel,
loc. Molinetto,
58023 Caldana Bivio

Tel   +39 0566 887100
Email   info@montebelli.com
Web   www.montebelli.com

Ethical Collection: Environment; Food. See page 211.

Price band: F

Locanda del Gallo

A restful, almost spiritual calm emanates from this wonderful home. In a medieval hamlet, the rustic locanda, all beams and terracotta, is a surprisingly green house. The saltwater pool clings to the side of a hill like a mirage underneath a huge lime tree – spectacular – and the jacuzzi is heated by solar thermals. Light, airy rooms have pale limewashed walls, exquisite reclaimed doors and carved hardwood furniture. Lighting is low-energy and supplied by renewables to supplement the sun's energy from thermals. Each bedroom is different, one almond-white with Italian country furniture, another pure white with wicker and Provençal prints; some have carved four-posters. Bathrooms are gorgeous, with deep baths (great for sharing!) and walk-in, glass-doored showers. A stunning veranda wraps itself around the house: doze off in a wicker armchair, sip a drink as the sun melts into the valley. Jimmy the cook conjures up dishes rich in flavour, with herbs and vegetables from the organic garden. He and his wife are part of the extended family; Paola and Irish are interesting and cultured. A perfect place. *Minimum stay three nights.*

Price	€120–€140. Half-board €75–€90 p.p. Suites €200–€240.
Rooms	9: 6 doubles, 3 suites for 4.
Meals	Dinner €28. Lunch €12. Wine from €10.
Closed	Rarely.
Directions	Exit E45 at Ponte Pattoli for Casa del Diavolo; for S Cristina 8km. 1st left, 100m after La Dolce Vita restaurant; continue to Locanda.

Ethical Collection: Environment; Food.
See page 211.

Price band: D

Paola Moro & Irish Breuer
Locanda del Gallo,
loc. Santa Cristina,
06020 Gubbio

Tel	+39 0759 229912
Email	info@locandadelgallo.it
Web	www.locandadelgallo.it

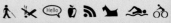

Agriturismo Madonna delle Grazie

There are rabbits, dogs, horses, ducks and hens, and Renato will pluck a cicada from an olive tree and show you how it 'sings'. Children who love animals will be in heaven. This is a real farm, not a hotel with a few animals wandering about, but agriturismo at its best, and you eat what they produce. The simple guest bedrooms in the 18th-century farmhouse are engagingly old-fashioned; all have a terrace or balcony with sweeping views – to Tuscany in one direction, Umbria in the other – and the bathrooms are unluxurious but spotless. The farm is fully organic and the food in the restaurant delicious; Renato's fruit and vegetables, olive oil, salami, chicken, plum jams, grappa and wine are home-produced or home-grown. There's also a big playground for children and table football in the house; little ones will love the Disney gnomes dotted around the picnic area. Book in for riding, archery or the San Casciano Terme spa (for which you get a discount). Renato has petitioned for community recycling, grey water feeds the garden and solar panels power the lights. A great little place.

Price	€100–€140.
Rooms	6 doubles.
Meals	Dinner €22. Wine €8–€12.
Closed	Rarely.
Directions	From A1 north: exit Chiusi-Chianciano, right to Chiusi & Città della Pieve. From A1 south: exit Fabro, turn left; left after 1km to Città della Pieve.

Signor Renato Nannotti
Agriturismo Madonna delle Grazie,
Madonna delle Grazie 6,
06062 Città della Pieve
Tel   +39 0578 299822
Email   info@madonnadellegrazie.it
Web   www.madonnadellegrazie.it

Ethical Collection: Environment; Food.
See page 211.

Price band: D

Agriturismo Contrada Durano

The zero-mile food philosophy is infectious. Spend a few days at this agriturismo and you'll never want to leave. Built in the late 18th-century as a refuge for monks, the hillside farm with glorious views has been lovingly restored by two generous, charming and eco-friendly owners: Englishman Jimmy and Italian Maria Concetta. No clutter, no fuss, just tiled floors, white walls, dark furniture, fine fabrics, cork insulation, compost loos, water preservation and a wood pellet boiler. The bedrooms are simple, peaceful, lovely; some are small, but the bar and sitting areas have ample space. If you're after a room with a view – of olive groves, vineyards and perched villages – ask for rooms 1 or 2. There's dinner most evenings, three dining areas in all and Maria Concetta's food makes the heart sing. The prosciutto and pecorino are local and organic, the bread is home-baked, the wine is home-grown. Soak in the garden jacuzzi, walk through wild flowers to the village of Smerillo, stock up with Durano bounty from the 'cantina' before you leave: olives, preserved apricots, wines from Le Marche. Bliss. *Minimum stay two nights.*

Price	€90.
Rooms	7 doubles.
Meals	Dinner with wine, €38.
Closed	Rarely.
Directions	A14 Ancona–Bari exit Porto San Giorgio for Amandola, 38km. 10km after Servigliano, sign on left; house 2km off road.

Ethical Collection: Environment; Food.
See page 211.

Price band: C

Maria Concetta Furnari
Agriturismo Contrada Durano,
Contrada Durano, 63020 Smerillo
Tel   +39 0734 786012
Email   info@contradadurano.it
Web   www.contradadurano.it

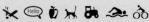

Locanda della Valle Nuova

In gentle, breeze-cooled hills, surrounded by ancient, protected oaks and on the road that leads to glorious Urbino, this 185-acre farm is an unusual, unexpectedly modern place whose owners' motto, that "one should tread lightly on the earth", colours every aspect of their lives. The cork-insulated farm, dotted with horses and two riding arenas, has been certified organic for nearly 25 years and nearly all of the delicious food and wine served by Signora Savini and her daughter Giulia is home-produced; the rest is sourced from local organic producers. In an area historically renowned for hunting, here it is forbidden, providing a haven for wild animals. Water is purified for drinking, showers are heated by the hot Italian sunshine, and prunings from the farm's woods, where truffles are gathered in autumn, feed a low-consumption wood stove to heat the house. It's worth asking for one of the bigger bedrooms, preferably with a view; all have bed linen and towels made from 100% natural fibres. With solar panels soon to be installed, La Locanda defines Italian eco agritourism. *Children over 12 welcome. Minimum stay three nights.*

Price	€108. Half-board €84 p.p. Apartments €680 per week.
Rooms	6 + 2: 5 doubles, 1 twin. 2 apartments for 2.
Meals	Dinner €30. Wine from €9.
Closed	Mid-November to May.
Directions	Exit Fano-Rome motorway at Acqualagna & Piobbico. Head towards Piobbico as far as Pole; right for Castellaro; on 3.5km, signed. Or, bus from Pesaro or Fano to Fermignano, owners will pick up.

Giulia Savini
Locanda della Valle Nuova,
La Cappella 14,
61033 Sagrata di Fermignano

Tel	+39 0722 330303
Email	info@vallenuova.it
Web	www.vallenuova.it

Ethical Collection: Environment; Food.
See page 211.

Price band: C

Casa Torre del Cornone

Bon viveur Alessio is the inspiration behind this environmental project. Off a narrow street, hanging high on the walls of a lovely medieval village, the house's big wooden doors opened to guests in 2006. Come not for unbridled luxury but for wholesome simplicity and a sensational location. High up, overseeing the green valley and the wooded hills, the house has glorious views in fine weather and feels cosy when the winds whistle and the snows drift. The tower of this (in parts ramshackle) mid 17th-century house was one of many that controlled the valley; now the building has entered the 21st century, with solar panels, cork-insulated walls and sustainable heating. In small simple bedrooms, original floor bricks and oak ceiling timbers remain, while plaster walls have been rendered with a traditional calcium and earth mix. Bedsteads have been welded by local craftsmen and bedcovers woven in muted colours. There are cookery weeks and landscape courses to inspire you and bikes to keep you fit, and the walk to the bar for breakfast is spectacular. A special place with an offbeat style.

Price	€60–€65. Singles €42–€45.
Rooms	7: 5 twins; 2 twins sharing bathroom.
Meals	Breakfast not included. Restaurants nearby.
Closed	Never.
Directions	From Rome, A24 to l'Aquila Est; SS17 to Pescara & Popoli; exit at fork with SS261 for San Demetrio & Molina; Fontecchio 15km. Call mobile 30 mins before arrival: meet in Piazza del Popolo, in front of Bar La Fontana.

Ethical Collection: Environment; Community.
See page 211.

Price band: C

Alessio di Giulio
Casa Torre del Cornone,
Cantone della Terra 22,
67020 Fontecchio
Tel   +39 0862 85441
Email   info@torrecornone.com
Web   www.torrecornone.com

Convento San Giorgio

In the early 17th century the hill of San Giorgio was donated by landowners to the Franciscan monks – as a deed 'good for the soul'. Stay in the monastery today and you'll find yourself leaving 21st-century materialism behind and focusing on "the things that matter". You won't be waited on here. High among forested hills overlooking the mountains life is basic and communal, but it is also wonderfully friendly and relaxed and you'll soon feel part of a working community. Whitewashed bedrooms are austere and clean, linen is provided only if requested, shower rooms are tiny and functional and a gong summons you to simple, mostly vegetarian, meals. Nanni is the presiding genius, naturally devoted to sustainable living. Originally from San Remo, where he set up a group for sustainable tourism, he's attempting to make San Giorgio entirely self-sufficient. Volunteer as a member of the Italian Greenpeace (Legambiente) during your stay: keep bees, rebuild ancient paths, seek out fresh water springs, protect bears living in the Sirente Velino National Park. *Annual European Eco-Village Conference held here.*

Price	Full-board €60 p.p.
	Half-board €45 p.p.
Rooms	22: 11 doubles; 6 twins;
	5 bunk rooms for 3-6.
Meals	Half- or full-board only.
	Restaurant 5-minute walk.
Closed	Mid-October to April.
Directions	A24 exit L'Aquila Est dir. Pescara. At
	1st x-roads right to Fontecchio; thro'
	Fontecchio; 4km, right for Tione degli
	Abruzzi; signed on left 1km before
	Goriano Valli.

Leonardo (Nanni) Laurent
Convento San Giorgio,
via Colle 1,
67020 Goriano Valli
Tel   +39 0862 88368
Email   info@conventosangiorgio.it
Web   www.conventosangiorgio.it

Ethical Collection: Environment;
Community; Food.
See page 211.

Price band: B

Modus Vivendi

Walkers, birdwatchers and outdoorsy types will love it here. Views stretch over rolling hills sprinkled with small towns while the mountains of the Majella National Park rise behind. Hospitable Emilia is a trained guide, an expert on birdlife and botany, and can suggest walks... she might even join you. Passionate about sustainability, she's restored her creamy stone house using local craftspeople and eco-friendly materials; there are ecological paints, wood-burning stoves, solar panels and recycled rainwater. Cool white and exposed stone walls, timbered ceilings and terracotta floors make rooms light and airy, while furnishings are traditional but uncluttered – wrought-iron or carved beds, richly coloured bedspreads, an antique armoire, a handsome chair. Bathrooms sparkle with chrome and pretty mosaics; all is fresh, new, pristine. The apartments have open-plan living areas with kitchens to one side, and terraces for dining. If you want to be spoiled, let Emilia cook for you, Abruzzese style, using produce local and organic. Dine under the pergola in summer and raise a glass of home-produced liqueur to those views.

Price	€60–€80.
	Apartments €540–€775 per week.
Rooms	5 + 2: 5 doubles. 2 apartments for 4.
Meals	Lunch & dinner from €20.
	Restaurant 5-minute drive.
Closed	Rarely.
Directions	A25 Rome-Pescara exit Scafa.
	Follow signs for Abbateggio for 10km;
	house signed.

Ethical Collection: Environment; Community; Food. See page 211.

Price band: C

Dario De Renzis
Modus Vivendi,
via Colle della Selva,
65020 Abbateggio

Tel   +39 0858 572136
Email   info@ecoalbergomodusvivendi.it
Web   www.ecoalbergomodusvivendi.it

Giravento

Built to environmental standards (local bricks, naturally treated wooden floors), surrounded by olive groves and orchards, Giravento is a paradise for birds, wild flowers, animals and green-sighted guests. Keen environmentalist Serena is socially minded, opening her doors to help shed light on rural development, biodiversity, ancient recipes, regional wine production and folk tradition. Bedrooms with private entrances are light, airy and thoroughly natural: stripped floors, eco lighting, solid country furniture, jewel-like splashes from rugs and bed throws. Heaps of space and walk-in showers, too. Flop around the pool or in the open-plan living area with views across the Taburno Camposauro regional park; snuggle up to the wood-burner in winter. Share a meal around the table and discover sweet Serena's passion for cooking with strict ecotarian principles: everything is local, seasonal, organic – Serena has spent years of careful research in her quest for earth-friendly sources. The results are delicious, so raise a glass and watch the magical fireflies perform. *Minimum stay two nights.*

Price	€90.
Rooms	3: 2 doubles, 1 triple.
Meals	Summer brunch €15. Dinner with wine, €30, by arrangement.
Closed	Rarely.
Directions	M'way Milan to Naples exit Caianello; on to Telesina on SS372 dir. Benavento. After 35km dir. Fondo Valle Isclero-Napoli, the S. Agata de' Goti. Exit for Melizzano, Amorosi, Solopaca, MEG Museo Engastronomico.

Serena Bova
Giravento,
vicinale Castagneto 7,
82030 Melizzano
Mobile   +39 347 2708153
Email   info@giravento.it
Web   www.giravento.it

Ethical Collection: Environment;
Community; Food.
See page 211.

Price band: C

Entry 169   Map 6

Azienda Agricola Le Tore Agriturismo

Vittoria is a vibrant presence and knows almost every inch of this wonderful coastline – its paths, its hill-perched villages, its secret corners. She sells award-winning organic olive oil, vinegar, preserves, nuts and lemons on her terraced five hectares, and she has this entry because of it. The cocks crow at dawn, distant dogs bark in the early hours and fireflies glimmer at night in the lemon groves. It's rural, the sort of place where you want to get up while there's still dew on the vegetables. The names of the bedrooms reflect their conversion from old farm buildings – 'Stalla', 'Fienile', 'Balcone' – and they are simply but solidly furnished. Excellent dinners are often served communally to guests; breakfast is taken at your own table under the pergola and could include raspberries, apple tart and fresh fruit juices. You must descend to coast level to buy your postcards, but this is a great spot from which to explore, and to walk – the CAI 'Alta via di Lattari' footpath is nearby. Le Tore is heaven to return to after a day's sightseeing, with views of the sea.

Price	€90. Apartment €700–€1,000 per week.
Rooms	6 + 1: 4 doubles, 1 twin, 1 family room for 4. Apartment for 5.
Meals	Dinner €25, by arrangement. Restaurant 5-min walk.
Closed	November to Palm Sunday.
Directions	A3 Naples-Palermo, exit Castellammare di Stabia for Positano. At x-roads for Positano, by restaurant Teresinella, sign for Sant'Agata; 7km, left on via Pontone; 1km.

Ethical Collection: Community; Food. See page 211.

Price band: C

Signora Vittoria Brancaccio
Azienda Agricola Le Tore Agriturismo,
via Pontone 43, Sant'Agata sui due Golfi,
80064 Massa Lubrense

Tel	+39 0818 080637
Email	info@letore.com
Web	www.letore.com

Lama di Luna – Biomasseria Agriturismo

The sister of Pietro's great-grandmother lived here until 1820; Pietro bought the farm in 1990, then discovered the family connection. It was "meant to be". Lama di Luna is a green dream, the most integrated organic farm in Italy: 200 hectares of olives and wines, 40 solar panels for heat and rain-harvested water, olive soaps and beds facing north, feng shui style. Pietro, who lives here with his family, is young, lively, charming, passionate about the environment and this serene place. The farm goes back 300 years and wraps its dazzling white self around a vast courtyard with a central bread oven, its 40 chimney pots a reminder of the many farm workers that once lived here; each bedroom, complete with fireplace and small window, once housed an entire family. Pietro searched high and low for the beds, the natural latex mattresses, the reclaimed wood for the doors. There's a library for reading and a veranda for sunsets and stars, with views that reach over flat farmland as far as the eye can see. Breakfast on homemade cakes and jams, orchard fruits and local cheeses. Remote, relaxing, memorable.

Price	€140–€150. Suites €200–€300.
Rooms	11: 9 twins/doubles, 2 suites.
Meals	Dinner with wine, €25. Restaurants 2km.
Closed	January-March.
Directions	A14 exit Canosa; Canosa-Andria, turn off for Montegrosso. After Montegrosso, 3.5km dir. Minervino. On left.

Pietro Petroni
Lama di Luna – Biomasseria Agriturismo,
loc. Montegrosso,
70031 Andria

Tel	+39 0883 569505
Email	info@lamadiluna.com
Web	www.lamadiluna.com

Ethical Collection: Environment; Food.
See page 211.

Price band: D

Entry 171   Map 6

Masseria Il Frantoio Agriturismo

So many ravishing things! An old, white house clear-cut against a blue sky, mysterious gardens, the scent of jasmine and a private beach five kilometres away. Owners Armando and Rosalba spent a year restoring this 17th-century house (built over a 6th-century oil press) after abandoning city life. Inside: sheer delight. A series of beautiful rooms, ranging from the fairytale (a froth of lace and toile) to the endearingly simple (madras bedcovers and old desks) and the formal (antique armoires and doughty, gilt-framed ladies)... an eclectic mix. Dinner is equally memorable – put your name down. Rosalba specialises in home-grown organic dishes accompanied by good local wines; Armando rings the courtyard bell at 8.30 and the feast begins, either in the arched dining room or the candlelit courtyard. There's an exterior white stone stairway climbing to a bedroom, an arched doorway swathed in wisteria. And there's a riding school on site, surrounded by olive groves and with a view of the sea. The organic farming demonstrations (open to the admiring public) are fantastic. *Minimum stay two nights.*

Price	€176–€220. Children €54–€64. Apartment €319–€350.
Rooms	8 + 1: 3 doubles, 2 triples, 3 family rooms. Apartment for 2-4.
Meals	Dinner with wine, €55, by arrangement. Cold supper, €31. Restaurant 5km.
Closed	Never.
Directions	Bari airport, E55 exit Pezze di Greco dir. Ostuni. On SS16, watch out for Ostuni km874 sign. Right into drive.

Ethical Collection: Community; Food.
See page 211.

Price band: E

Silvana Caramia
Masseria Il Frantoio Agriturismo,
SS 16km 874,
72017 Ostuni

Tel	+39 0831 330276
Email	prenota@masseriailfrantoio.it
Web	www.masseriailfrantoio.it

Palazzo Bacile di Castiglione

The palazzo's 16th-century walls dominate Spongano's Piazza Bacile and, just as in times of old, the family is an influential part of the community. With this generation 'green' holds sway, thanks to Sarah, English wife of the charming *barone*. A campaigner for improved picking up of litter and the use of solar energy, she offers Bacile's sun-powered apartments, elegantly spread over three floors, as a prime example. On the first floor is the largest, its four bedrooms opening off a vaulted hall with terraces – beige check sofas, a grand piano, choice fabrics, new four-posters, wardrobes dwarfed by lofty ceilings. a fireplace filled with estate logs. The simple outbuildings at the end of the long garden are similarly swish inside: olive wood tables, big lamps, framed engravings, books and CDs, kitchens for cooks. The garden is lovely, all orange trees and wisteria, secluded walkways and corners, old pillars and an impressive pool; at twilight, scops owls chime like bells. Beyond lie the baroque splendours of Lecce, Gallipoli and Otranto – and the coast. Borrow the bikes!
Minimum stay four nights. Metered air conditioning.

Price	€900–€2,770 per week.	
Rooms	7 apartments: 2 for 2, 3 for 4, 1 for 6, 1 for 8.	
Meals	Restaurant 500m.	
Closed	Never.	
Directions	Lecce N16 exit Nociglia (after Maglie); to Surano, then Spongano; cross railway into centre; on Piazza Bacile, entrance to left of Farmacia. Please call Giuseppe (mob: +39 347 6524477) if lost.	

	Sarah & Alessandro Bacile di Castiglione Palazzo Bacile di Castiglione, 73038 Spongano	Ethical Collection: Environment. See page 211.
Tel	+39 0832 351131	
Email	albadica@hotmail.com	Price band: B
Web	www.palazzobacile.it	

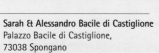

Hotel Villa Schuler

Late in the 19th century, Sig. Schuler's great-grandfather travelled by coach from Germany and built his house high above the Ionian Sea. He built on a grand scale and he chose the site well – the views of the Bay of Naxos and Mount Etna are gorgeous. When he died in 1905, Great Grandmama decided to let out some rooms; the villa has been a hotel ever since. Though restored and brought up to date, it still has an old, elegant charm and a relaxed, peaceful atmosphere. Lavish organic breakfasts are served in the low-energy chandelier'd breakfast room or out on the terrace. Bedrooms vary; some have beautifully tiled floors, antique furniture and stone balconies, while the more modern top-floor suites have beamed ceilings and large terraces. All come with organic linen, jacuzzi showers heated by solar panels, heating from biomass and views out to sea – or over the vast, subtropical garden scented with jasmine. Hidden away behind a stone arch is a delightful, very private little apartment. A path leads through the gardens and out into the town's pedestrianised Corso Umberto. Lovely. *Minimum stay two-four nights (mid-high season).*

Price	€107-€206. Apartment €250 for 2, €390 for 4.
Rooms	26 + 1: 17 doubles, 5 suites, 4 triples. Apt for 2-4.
Meals	Breakfast included for self-caterers. Restaurants 100m (special prices for Schuler guests).
Closed	Mid-November to February.
Directions	A18 exit Taormina; 3km; at 'Lumbi' car park into 'Monte Tauro' tunnel; around 'Porta Catania' car park to Piazza S. Antonio; right at P.O. into via Pietro Rizzo; right into via Roma.

Ethical Collection: Environment.
See page 211.

Price band: E

Christine Voss & Gerhard Schuler
Hotel Villa Schuler,
Piazzetta Bastione,
Via Roma, 98039 Taormina

Tel	+39 0942 23481
Email	info@hotelvillaschuler.com
Web	www.hotelvillaschuler.com

Agriturismo Sillitti

Drive through rolling farmland, up past the olive groves, until you can climb no further. This is it: stunning 360 degree views over the island and, on a clear day, Mount Etna in the distance. Silvia's family have farmed for generations. She's passionately organic – grows almonds, wheat, vegetables, olives (stay for November's harvest, a joy) – and shares her recipes and her kitchen garden; she gives organic tours, too. The farmhouse is new and biomass heated, its apartments bright and simple, furnished in cheery style with cream floor tiles and new pine. Open-plan living areas include tiny kitchens for rustling up simple meals; rooms won't win design prizes but are spotless with views; hot water is solar spiced. Silvia and Bruno (a doctor in Palermo) are charming – you'll be won over by their warmth and her cooking. There's homemade bread, cake and jam at breakfast, and a feast of Sicilian dishes at dinner. After exploring the island – don't miss the Roman villa at Piazza Armerina – return to a garden with saltwater pool, terrace, shady pavilion, and those breathtaking views. *Minimum stay two nights.*

Price	€80. Apartments €460–€920 per week.
Rooms	5 + 3: 5 doubles.
	3 apartments for 2–5.
Meals	Dinner with wine, €25.
	Restaurants 5km.
Closed	Rarely.
Directions	A19 exit Caltanissetta. After SS640, dir. Agrigento; after 50km right for Serradifalco; 300m then left; phone for further directions.

	Silvia Sillitti
	Agriturismo Sillitti,
	Contrada Grotta D'Acqua,
	93100 Caltanissetta
Tel	+39 0934 930733
Email	info@sillitti.it
Web	www.sillitti.it

Ethical Collection: Food.
See page 211.

Price band: C

Ionian Eco Villages

In green and sunny Zante, under pine-scented hills, strolling distance from miles of sand, is a friendly collection of villas, apartments and stone cottages. Surrounded by olive groves, in lush gardens of citrus and bougainvillea, they make a bright splash. But it is the warmth of Yannis's welcome and his commitment to conservation that really stand out. The Gerakas peninsula, now part of the marine park, is one of the last nesting sites of the loggerhead sea turtle and Yannis has battled impressively to keep mass tourism at bay. These comfortable homes, many solar- or wind-powered, have sea views, timbered ceilings, cool tiles, simple kitchens, open showers, a family ornament here, a touch of kitsch there. The cracking sound of the locals taking pot shots at the birds might puncture the tranquillity but you are in rural Greece. Come in spring or autumn for meadows of wild flowers and venture out with volunteers in a summer's dawn for the unforgettable sight of hatchlings on the beach. Walking safaris, too, and a sea turtle rehabilitation centre on its way. *Discount for guests willing to volunteer.*

Ethical Collection: Environment.
See page 211.

Price band: C

Price	£440–£546 (sterling) per week for 2.
Rooms	1 cottage for 5, 1 farmhouse for 6, 3 villas for 3, 3 studios for 3, 4 apts for 3, 4 apts for 4.
Meals	Basic breakfast included. Restaurants in Gerakas village.
Closed	October–April.
Directions	14km from Zakynthos town signed Vassilikos & Gerakas. Follow final sign for Gerakas 1km from site. Bus from Zakynthos.

Helen King & Yannis Vardakastanis
Ionian Eco Villages,
Gerakas Taverna,
29100 Vassilkos, Zakynthos

Tel	+44 (0)871 7115065
Email	rachelhallam@relaxing-holidays.com
Web	www.relaxing-holidays.com

We've recently launched our series-wide Ethical Collection, which celebrates owners whose places go the extra mile, and who take the steps that most people have not yet taken, in one or more of the following areas:

• Environment Those making great efforts to reduce the environmental impact of their Special Place. We expect more than energy-saving light bulbs and recycling – in this part of the Collection you will find owners who make their own natural cleaning products, properties with solar hot water and biomass boilers, the odd green roof and a good measure of green elbow grease.

• Community Given to owners who use their property to play a positive role in their local and wider community. For example, by making a contribution from every guest's bill to a local fund, or running pond-dipping courses for local school children on their farm.

• Food Awarded to owners who make a real effort to source local or organic food, or to grow their own. We look for those who have gone out of their way to strike up relationships with local producers or to seek out organic suppliers. It is easier for an owner on a farm to produce their own eggs than for someone in the middle of a city, so we take this into account.

How it works

In our other books owners can decide whether or not to apply for these awards; to be included in this book, they must have gained at least one award – and many have

two, or even all three; details are shown on each entry page.

Owners decide which categories to apply in, and fill out a detailed questionnaire asking demanding questions about their activities in the chosen areas. (You can download a full list of the questions from our website.)

We then review each questionnaire carefully before deciding whether or not to give the award(s). The final decision is subjective; it is based not only on whether an owner ticks 'yes' to a question but also on the detailed explanation that accompanies each 'yes' or 'no' answer. For example, an owner who has tried as hard as possible to install solar water-heating panels, but has failed because of strict conservation planning laws, will be given some credit for their effort (as long as they are doing other things in this area).

There is stacks more information on our website, sawdays.co.uk. You can read the answers each owner has given in support of their application, and get a more detailed idea of what they are doing in each area.

We have tried to be as rigorous as possible and have made sure the questions are demanding. We've learned a lot from our owners across Europe and are proud to share their knowledge with you. The Ethical Collection is still a new initiative for us, and we'd love to know what you think about it – write to us or email us at ethicalcollection@sawdays.co.uk.

Jargon is run-of-the-(sustainable)-mill in Eco Ville so, if you're wondering who practices 'ecotarianism', why the sign to your loo has 'compost' as a prefix or what a 'reed bed system' is, read on.

Air-source heat pump – a heat pump that uses the outside air as a heat source or heat sink to heat or cool an interior space. See also 'geothermal heating'.

Bio – short for 'biological', and used as a prefix to indicate that living matter is involved. Note that organic food is *produits biologiques* in French, *Bioprodukte* in German.

Biodynamic farming – organic farming with a twist: plants are sown according to an astronomical calendar, and fermented herbal and mineral preparations are used as compost additives and field sprays.

Photo: Eco Hotel Cristallina, entry 91

Biomass – biological material that can be used as fuel (eg. wood).

Compost loo/dry wc – a clever waterless system that converts human waste into a useful compost through the natural breakdown of organic matter into its essential minerals.

Carbon-neutral – having no net carbon emissions or, more contentiously, when any carbon emitted is replaced through the creation of carbon sinks, such as newly planted trees. [Carbon-negative is used to describe places that generate more (renewable) energy than they consume; the excess is usually sold back to the 'grid'.]

Eco – short for 'ecological'; as a prefix it describes anything that is environmentally sustainable.

Ecotarian – someone who sources food from environmentally sustainable or ethical sources, eg. local (low carbon journey to the plate), organic, fairtrade.

Geothermal heating – use of the heat stored in the ground; a ground-source heat pump extracts this heat to warm buildings.

Grey water – water from last night's washing-up or this morning's bath. Grey water is often used on the garden, hence the need to use environmentally friendly washing-up liquids and shampoos.

Heat exchange – a method of extracting heat from one source (eg. air leaving a building) and transferring it to another to make the most efficient use of energy.

Non-VOC paints – paints that contain no volatile organic compounds (chemicals whose fumes contribute to global warming, and are sometimes linked to cancer).

Organic – items grown, reared or manufactured according to specific minimum production standards; outside the EU exact requirements for organic certification vary, but generally conventional pesticides and artifical fertilizers must not be used. Not to be confused with *organico* in Italian or *organique* in French, both of which simply mean 'something that grows'. See also 'bio'.

Permaculture – an agricultural system that places the undisturbed 'permanence' of ecosystems at its heart, creating a balance between human and ecological needs.

Rainwater harvesting – collection and storage of rainwater in tanks, for use in showers, wcs and gardens.

Reed bed sewage system – system of reed-filled ponds in which natural micro-organisms filter and clean sewage.

Renewable ('green') energy – energy generated by harnessing naturally occurring, infinite sources of energy, eg. wind, sunlight, water, geothermal heat.

Slow Food – global movement based on the philosophy that food tastes better when grown organically, harvested locally and eaten in season. The movement champions artisan-producers.

Solar thermal power – a way of using solar energy to heat water, usually using a rooftop system of fluid-filled tubes to collect and move the heat.

Solar photovoltaic (PV) panels – technology that converts sunshine directly into electricity.

Photo: Ca' del Rocolo, entry 155

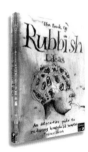

The Book of Rubbish Ideas
An interactive, room by room, guide to reducing household waste
£6.99

This guide to reducing household waste and stopping wasteful behaviour is essential reading for all those trying to lessen their environmental impact.

Ban the Plastic Bag
A Community Action Plan
£4.99

In May 2007 Modbury in South Devon became Britain's first plastic bag free town. This book tells the Modbury story, but uses it as a call to action, entreating every village, town and city in the country to follow Modbury's example and... BAN THE PLASTIC BAG.

One Planet Living
£4.99

"Small but meaningful principles that will improve the quality of your life."
Country Living

Also available in the Fragile Earth series:

The Little Food Book   £6.99
"This is a really big little book. It will make your hair stand on end" *Jonathan Dimbleby*

The Little Money Book   £6.99
"Anecdotal, humorous and enlightening, this book will have you sharing its gems with all your friends" *Permaculture Magazine*

To order any of the books in the Fragile Earth series call +44 (0)1275 395431 or visit www.fragile-earth.com

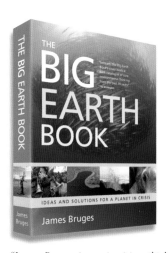

"James Bruges is an inspiring thinker"
Green World

The Big Earth Book
Updated paperback edition
£12.99

We all know the Earth is in crisis. We should know that it is big enough to sustain us if we can only mobilise politicians and economists to change course now. Expanding on the ideas developed in *The Little Earth Book*, this book explores environmental, economic and social ideas to save our planet. It helps us understand what is happening to the planet today, exposes the actions of corporations and the lack of action of governments, weighs up new technologies, and champions innovative and viable solutions. Tackling a huge range of subjects – it has the potential to become the seminal reference book on the state of the planet – it's the one and only environmental book you really need.

"An excellent debunking of the myths that justify inaction" *The Ecologist*

What About China? £6.99
Answers to this and other awkward questions about climate change

"What is the point of doing anything when China opens a new power station every week?" All of us are guilty of making excuses not to change our lifestyles especially when it comes to global warming and climate change. *What About China?* explains that all the excuses we give to avoid making changes that will reduce our carbon footprint and our personal impact on the environment, are exactly that, excuses! Through clear answers, examples, facts and figures the book illustrates how any changes we make now will have an effect, both directly and indirectly, on climate change.

Wheelchair-accessible

At least one bedroom and bathroom accessible for wheelchair users. Phone for details.

Good for vegetarians

Good vegetarian dinner options (arrange in advance at B&Bs).

On a budget?

Double room for £70/€100 or under.

Norway 113
Sweden 119 • 121
Portugal 131 • 132
Spain 133 • 134 • 136 • 137 •
138 • 140 • 141 • 142 • 143 •
146 • 147 • 149 • 151
Italy 152 • 153 • 154 • 155 •
156 • 157 • 158 • 159 • 163 •
164 • 166 • 169
Greece 176

Suitable for large groups
The whole building can be hired for an event.

Britain 3 • 7 • 9 • 12 • 13 •
14 • 16 • 24 • 27 • 30 • 31 •
33 • 34 • 37
Northern Ireland 44
Ireland 46 • 47 • 49 • 51
Belgium 55 • 58
France 59 • 61 • 66 • 69 • 70 •
72 • 76 • 77 • 78 • 82 • 84 •
85 • 86 • 88 • 89 • 90
Switzerland 91 • 92 • 93 • 95
Austria 98 • 102
Germany 103 • 107 • 108
Finland 111
Norway 113 • 114 • 117
Sweden 118 • 119 • 120 •
123 • 124
Iceland 128
Portugal 129 • 131 • 132
Spain 133 • 134 • 137 • 143 •
145 • 146 • 147 • 149 • 151
Italy 152 • 153 • 156 • 157 •
158 • 159 • 160 • 161 • 163 •
164 • 165 • 166 • 173

No car?
These owners are within 10 miles of a bus/coach/train station and owner can arrange collection.

Britain 1 • 2 • 3 • 6 • 7 • 8 • 9 •
10 • 13 • 14 • 16 • 17 • 19 •
20 • 23 • 24 • 26 • 27 • 29 •
30 • 31 • 32 • 34 • 35 • 36 •
37 • 38 • 41 • 42 • 43
Northern Ireland 45
Ireland 47 • 48 • 49 • 51
Belgium 54 • 55 • 56 • 57 • 58
France 59 • 61 • 62 • 65 • 67 •
68 • 69 • 70 • 71 • 72 • 74 •
75 • 77 • 79 • 80 • 81 • 82 •
83 • 85 • 86 • 88 • 89
Switzerland 91 • 92 • 93 • 94 •
95 • 96
Austria 98 • 99 • 100 • 101 •
102
Germany 103 • 104 • 105 •
106 • 107 • 108 • 109
Finland 110 • 111
Norway 113 • 114 • 115 •
116 • 117
Sweden 118 • 119 • 120 •
121 • 122 • 123 • 124
Denmark 125 • 126 • 127
Portugal 131 • 132
Spain 133 • 135 • 137 • 140 •
141 • 142 • 144 • 146 • 148 •
149 • 150 • 151
Italy 153 • 154 • 155 • 159 •
163 • 165 • 166 • 167 • 170 •
171 • 172 • 173 • 174

Quick reference indices

Triodos ⊛ Bank

Triodos Bank's motives are as decent as one can find: it lends only to organisations and companies that it considers to be making a positive contribution to the planet and the community. Here, a little of the bank's refreshingly different approach to money is explained.

Money is in constant flow. Like electricity, you can't benefit directly from it, only from what it can do for you. We've become used to it being reduced to numbers on a page, almost a commodity with a pure numeric meaning. Newspapers, journals and adverts list reams of percentages earned, or paid, for money that can be borrowed, saved or invested.

Where money itself is the product, it's easy to believe that nothing exists other than the rate of return. We're encouraged by the media, and conventional wisdom, to chase the highest interest rates. We don't need to think about this money, or who might be bearing the consequences of our earning sometimes unfeasibly high rates of return. By entrusting money to a bank, we wash our hands of it. It's just a mechanism for multiplying money until we need to use it.

In a global financial system obsessed by the 'fast buck', maximising profit in the short term, there is a growing movement of ethical organisations, like Triodos Bank, that takes a more holistic view. A solid banking sector is needed to finance solutions to the real problems we face, especially climate change. The banks should respond, not least because they can. Instead of generating artificial profits from complex financial instruments and unacceptable risks, banks are in a unique position to facilitate lasting change.

Triodos exists to make money work for people and the planet, reconnecting savers with the impact of their investment. That Triodos has been able to side-step the worst impact of the current financial crisis, and prosper despite it, is not a matter of luck. As the core of its banking, it finances sustainable businesses delivering clear social, environmental and cultural benefits.

Triodos Bank was conceived in 1968, when four friends – an economist, a professor, a consultant and a banker – formed a study group. These men, inspired by student protests round the world and the work of Austrian social thinker Rudolf Steiner, debated how money could be handled in a socially-conscious way. They wanted finance to act in a way that values community, culture and the environment, as well as profit. Today, Triodos is Europe's leading ethical bank, with funds under management of over £3 billion and branches in the UK, The Netherlands, Belgium and Spain. Through its pioneering microfinance work, providing finance for millions of poorer people in the developing world, the Bank's influence is truly global.

Triodos has much in common with any other bank, lending out the money that people deposit with it. In return, it provides a safe home for savers' money and a return on their investment. What sets Triodos Bank apart is how and to whom it lends this money. Triodos only finances organisations working to benefit people and the environment. What an enterprise sets out to do, and what motivates the people behind it, are the Bank's first consideration, examined before a loan's financial viability is even considered. The projects that do make the grade are in areas ranging from renewable energy and recycling to fair trade and organic farming. Some are national names, including Ecotricity and Cafédirect, while the impact of others is felt more locally, like community groups and village shops. There's even an eco-publisher or two in there. A loan from Triodos Bank helped Alastair Sawday's dream of having one of the UK's most environmentally friendly offices become a reality in 2006 – with super-insulation, underfloor heating, a wood pellet boiler, solar panels and a rainwater tank.

To show that it really puts its money where its mouth is, Triodos Bank publishes an annual list of everyone it lends money to. Savers can see how Triodos is using their investment, and can understand the benefits their money brings. Triodos is the only commercial bank in the UK to do this. With recent examples of conventional banks funding projects including the Nam Theun 2 Hydropower Project in Laos, despite significant negative environmental and social impacts, it's easy to see why some banks would be uneasy with the notion of making public their loan book. And while most money held by conventional banks probably isn't doing any harm, Triodos Bank savers know their money is actively doing good. It connects them, in a simple and practical way, to the enterprises that they want to see flourishing.

Triodos Bank is delighted to support this book.

Triodos Bank only finances organisations that benefit people or the environment – from inspiring renewable energy projects to organic farms. And it is done with money deposited by thousands of savers across the UK. If you'd like to be one them, visit www.triodos.co.uk or call free on 0500 008 720.

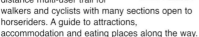
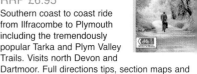

Photo: Engholm Husky Lodge, entry 113

① France: Rhône Valley – Alps   **②** B&B

③ Chalet Châtelet

④ The lush Vallée d'Abondance envelops this pretty new pine chalet, whose owners fizz with enthusiasm for the life they share with guests. There are oak floors, soft shapes, high ceilings, reclaimed furniture and works by Suzie's arty family. Pascal and Suzie built their home with the aim of living in utter comfort while having zero impact on the planet. Their mission was to integrate an eco house into the vernacular, orientate for the best views and maximise solar potential. Hand-chiselled local logs packed with lambs wool form one part; honeycomb bricks and local stone set in lime another. Warmth comes from a 'stone with soul' Finnish stove, clever insulation (that also includes cork and hemp) and solar panels (photovoltaic and thermal). Expect cultured chat in the intimate dining room, where Suzie serves organic meals cooked on the log-burning range. Produce is as local as can be. Wake from a deep sleep amidst soft organic linen to stunning views; shower with French natural soaps in dreamy bathrooms; gaze at mountains you plan to climb or ski that day. A home from home embraced by green. *Ask about ski & activity packages.*

Price	€90–€190.	**⑤**
Rooms	4: 2 doubles, 2 triples.	**⑥**
Meals	Dinner with wine, €30.	**⑦**
Closed	Rarely.	**⑧**
Directions	Thonon D902 for Morzine & Vallée	**⑨**
	d'Abondance. After 2nd tunnel, left	
	at r'bout D22 for Vallée d'Abondance	
	& Châtel. After La Solitude, right onto	
	D32 Bonnevaux. At church fork left;	
	chalet 300m on left.	

⑩ Ethical Collection: Environment; Food.
See page 211.

Pascal & Suzie Immediato
Chalet Châtelet,
Route d'Abondance,
74360 Bonnevaux

⑪ Price band: E

Tel	+33 (0)4 50 73 69 48
Email	p.s.immediato@orange.fr
Web	www.chalet-chatelet.com

⑫ Entry 80   Map 2    **⑬**